# Relationships That Bless

# Relationships That Bless

by
Isaac D. Martin

**Rod and Staff Publishers, Inc.**
*P.O. Box 3, Hwy. 172
Crockett, Kentucky 41413
Telephone: (606) 522-4348*

*Copyright 2004*
*Rod and Staff Publishers, Inc.*
*Crockett, Kentucky 41413*

Printed in U.S.A.

ISBN 0-7399-2318-8

Catalog no. 2375

3   4   5   6   7   —   18   17   16   15   14   13   12   11   10   09

## *Table of Contents*

Introduction ........................................9

1. The Basis for Good Relationships ......................15
2. Relationships Within the Family .......................21
3. Relationships Within the Church ......................59
4. Relationships Within the School .......................99
5. Relationships Within the Community ..................123
6. Christian Employee and Employer Relationships ........133

# *Introduction*

"And as ye would that men should do to you, do ye also to them likewise" (Luke 6:31). This, of course, is the Golden Rule. Jesus was teaching His disciples to measure the way they treated others by the way they wanted to be treated.

But near the end of Jesus' pilgrimage here, He gave them a measuring stick having even finer markings. He said to His disciples, "A new commandment I give unto you, That ye love one another; *as I have loved you,* that ye also love one another" (John 13:34). He called them, and us, to love with a Godlike love that is impossible outside of the new-birth experience. We cannot relate to other people in a Christian way unless we are indeed Christians and have the Lord's life and love within us.

How important are relationships? What did Jesus say? "Therefore if thou bring thy gift to the altar, and there rememberest that thy brother hath ought against thee; leave there thy gift before the altar, and go thy way; first be reconciled to thy brother, and then come and offer thy gift" (Matthew 5:23, 24). Relationships are just that important. True, we cannot build a relationship with God by building relationships with people. But we can ruin a relationship with God by ruining relationships with people.

Relationships are important because human experience is full of them. A little baby first observes the way his father and mother relate to him. He soon learns what type of behavior brings favor. In most families, sooner or later, he needs to learn to relate to brothers, sisters, grandparents, uncles, aunts, and neighbors. As the child's world enlarges, so does the number of relationships that affect him. Most of us, no matter how old, are still enlarging our circle of acquaintances.

Good relationships are important to consider because we must maintain them. They depend upon the proper input from each side. We, not just the other person, have the capacity to imagine, suspect, fear, trust, love, or hate. Furthermore, we have some ability to keep up, suspend, or terminate a relationship. When a good relationship is spoiled, we usually prefer to think the other person spoiled it. Maybe so. Maybe we can escape blame. But we cannot escape responsibility. The mandate "As much as lieth in you, live peaceably with all men" (Romans 12:18) still rings in our ears.

Since relationships are important, bad ones must be broken. When a sinner is converted, he must limit or break off many of his former associations and establish new ones among God's people. Even among religious people, we need to decide whether a relationship is beneficial or detrimental. This calls for carefulness because Jesus said, "Judge not, that ye be not judged" (Matthew 7:1). However, in the same chapter He said, "Beware of false prophets.... By their fruits ye shall know them." This teaches us that we do need to discern between the true and the false and make proper choices.

Relationships are important because they put a Christian in touch with the world. Although the Christian is separate from the world and is translated into the kingdom of Christ, he is still very much a part of his community. Although he has obeyed the call "Come out from among them, and be ye separate" (2 Corinthians 6:17), yet he carries a compassionate love for the souls of lost men and women. He is like Jesus, who was "separate from sinners" (Hebrews 7:26) but at the same time "a friend of publicans and sinners" (Matthew 11:19). Only by establishing relationships with people in the world can Christians "save" any of them from the world.

Relationships are important because they are always changing. Alliances develop and later crumble. People seem to easily switch from one job to another. Many shift from one church to another or even start one of their own because of difficult relationships. At every turn in the

## Introduction

road, a lesson about relating to people awaits us. We are only human, and we have a good bit to learn.

We can learn from Jesus how to relate properly to the varied people we meet. The Sermon on the Mount (Matthew 5, 6 and 7) deals largely with relationships. What Jesus said in that sermon is basically this: the Christian's way of relating to others rises above that which is natural. We are called to be like God! "Be ye therefore perfect, even as your Father which is in heaven is perfect" (Matthew 5:48). The Spirit of God makes this possible. Christians remain sweet and unruffled under provocation. They repent when they fail to love and be Christlike. They even surround themselves with those who care enough to confront friends when they do wrong.

The more valuable a relationship is, the greater will be its intensity. Valuable relationships involve listening to what people have to say, trusting them, obeying them if they are responsible to guide us, and joining them in their joys and sorrows. God does not intend that all relationships carry this much intensity. Obviously, some relationships must be given more attention than others, but a Christian should cultivate at least a few close relationships.

The Christian resists the temptation to judge people by first impressions. Children do that, and some of us know what it is like to be the victim of a tiny tot's hasty rejection. We must first learn to know about people. From that knowledge we decide if we want to know more about them. Even if people disappoint us, spiritual love keeps us from writing them off as unfit for further friendship.

Of course, we must be prudent and discerning. Christians, above all people, are vulnerable in relationships. We are as sheep in the midst of wolves. This causes us to approach any relationship with a bit of caution. But with the Spirit of God and the Word guiding us, we can fearlessly relate to people with a confidence in God that the world cannot know. We are willing to be hurt, disappointed, betrayed, and even rejected by former friends. We refuse to yield to fear lest we greatly hinder our usefulness. We let the love of God govern us instead.

Relating to other people might seem complicated or even frightening sometimes. But God always has a right way for us when we seek His will in our relationships.

This book is dedicated to serious Christians facing the struggle of maintaining holy relationships. A special thanks goes to David L. Martin for his extensive editorial work and his additon of many practical illustrations that give meaning to the teachings.

*Chapter One*

# *The Basis for Good Relationships*

"It is not good," God said, "that the man should be alone" (Genesis 2:18). This was no new thought to God. He had created man with the need for companionship. And so, in a very special way, God provided a companion. "And the rib, which the Lord God had taken from man, made he a woman, and brought her unto the man. And Adam said, This is now bone of my bones, and flesh of my flesh: she shall be called Woman, because she was taken out of Man" (Genesis 2:22, 23). Thus began the most intimate relationship of humanity. God designed marriage to provide a wholesome climate for learning to interact with others.

God shared in this relationship. He walked "in the garden in the cool of the day" (Genesis 3:8), and the implication is strong that He habitually spent time in the Garden in fellowship with Adam and Eve.

But Adam and Eve's disobedience broke their relationship with God. The voice of God caused them to flee and hide. Sin not only affected their relationship with God, but it also changed their way of relating to each other. When Adam said, "The woman whom thou gavest to be with me," he was lashing out in two directions at once—blaming his wife and blaming God, who gave her to him. This was the beginning of strained relationships among humans.

God had a solution for this. He taught His people how to have a right relationship with Him, though that relationship was not so close as Adam and Eve had once enjoyed. On that basis—a right relationship with God—they could once again relate comfortably to each other. Finally, God sent Jesus, the foundation for true Christian relationships. When we believe in Jesus Christ and repent of our sins, God makes us new creatures, and the Spirit of Christ sheds His love abroad in our hearts. Then we have the power to love everyone, even those who have made themselves our enemies.

While every true Christian has this love, it is not perfected in us. We all have many things to learn about the function of Christlike love. This book should help us to learn them. So should the stresses and surprises of life that God has in store for us. Always we will come back to the same conclusion: the more we yield ourselves to Christ, the greater will be the glow of His love in us, and the better we will get along with people.

## A. Learning From God

What can we learn about relating to each other from God's example?

Consider the unselfishness of God. The Father, Son, and Holy Spirit have perfect union. Why? Because they obviously live for and love each other. One particle of selfishness would ruin the perfect harmony, but there is no selfishness. Jesus did not consider it robbery to be equal with God, since He is God. However, out of love, not only to us but also to His Father, He made Himself of no reputation and submitted Himself to death on the cross to be our Saviour (Philippians 2:1–11). "I do always those things that please [God]," Jesus said (John 8:29).

We can say, "But that is love among the Godhead, and we are not God. Therefore we cannot have that perfection of relationships." Why then did Jesus tell us to be perfect even as our Father in heaven is perfect? He spoke this in the context of loving our enemies (Matthew 5:43–48). We cannot love as deeply as God can, but there is a perfection of love that we can enjoy. When the Holy Spirit gives us God's supernatural love, we can love everyone, even those difficult to love.

## The Basis For Good Relationships

Consider also the order of God—not His orderliness but His established order of authority. "My Father is greater than I," Jesus said in John 14:28, showing that He had found His own place in God's order. Jesus also said of the Holy Spirit, "He shall not speak of himself; but whatsoever he shall hear, that shall he speak" (John 16:13). In the Trinity, the Father might be thought of as the chairman, and the Son and Spirit work together with Him.

To relate properly to others, we too must understand God's established order. He created us to be followers. We all need leaders. Even the man who seems to be at the top has God above him. If he does not do what God intends for him to do, he will be removed in God's time. David, king in waiting, understood God's established order. Given the opportunity to destroy King Saul, he refused, saying, "Who can stretch forth his hand against the LORD's anointed, and be guiltless?" (1 Samuel 26:9).

For a negative example, think of Korah (Numbers 16). Korah did not understand God's order. Having become a little famous, he surrounded himself with admirers who made him feel even more important. He then accused Moses and Aaron of lifting themselves above the congregation. Moses understood the seriousness of what Korah was doing and fell on his face. Korah and his friends, sad to say, did not. God, to re-establish His order, made the earth open up and swallow them.

The problem of important men exalting themselves did not end with God's swift judgment on Korah. It continues today. Men become a little prominent for some reason; then they look with disfavor on those whom God has put over them. They decide that they must be at least equal to the ones over them in leadership. This causes them to accuse their leaders rather than supporting them. This wreaks havoc, especially when it happens in the church.

Consider finally the humility of God. Nowhere was this more evident than when the Son of God came to earth as a helpless baby. He grew up under human parents and was subject to them.

Jesus did one thing that we cannot do. He "made himself of no reputation" (Philippians 2:7). We cannot lay aside a reputation we do not have. But we can do this: We can lay aside the reputation we always *thought* we had. We can sometimes let others be over us, and like Jesus, we can be "subject unto them" (Luke 2:51). We have more reason to do this than Jesus ever did.

God has made us all different, and rightly so. We have no business setting ourselves up as the standard by which others must be judged. We must not assume that if someone else has more authority than we do, he has too much; or that if someone is stronger than we, he is musclebound; or that if he can think farther than we can, he is too wise for his own good; or that if he fills a place we forgot to fill, he must be self-important. Let the humble example of Christ be the pattern for everyone, especially ourselves.

Once it is settled that we have no reputation to protect, we can relax. Being perfectly free from ourselves, we can love as God does, and we can submit to His order. Relationships will then prove a blessing wherever we go.

## B. Walking With God

Enoch walked with God. Abraham was a friend to God. God talked with Moses as a man speaks with a friend. Many other Bible characters enjoyed intimate relationships with God. It should be evident that the King of all creation is a friendly God.

Down through the centuries, men and women have loved and served God. They have found satisfaction in walking with the Lord. The *Church and Sunday School Hymnal* has the following hymn, which comes to us from a time of persecution. It portrays the loving relationship God can have with us.

### My Lord and I

I have a friend so precious, so very dear to me,
He loves me with such tender love, loves me so faithfully;
I could not live apart from Him, I long to feel Him nigh,
And so we dwell together, *my precious Lord and I.*

## The Basis For Good Relationships

Sometimes I'm faint and weary, He knows that I am weak,
And, as He bids me lean on Him, His help I gladly seek;
He leads me in the paths of light, beneath a sunny sky,
And so we walk together, *my precious Lord and I.*

I tell Him all my sorrows, I tell Him all my joys,
I tell Him all that pleases me, I tell Him what annoys;
He tells me what I ought to do, He tells me what to try,
And so we talk together, *my precious Lord and I.*

He knows how I am longing some precious soul to win
Back to the ways of righteousness from weary paths of sin;
He bids me tell His wondrous love and why He came to die,
And so we work together, *my precious Lord and I.*

    Christians should learn to think of God as someone near. Certainly it is right that we think of God as the great, exalted one in control of the entire universe. But we should also think of Him as being great enough to take a personal interest in everyone. He is one with whom we can share what annoys or pleases us.

    In light of this, we can be frank with God even about our bad attitudes toward people. We need not cover up our true feelings; God sees them anyhow. One woman who claimed to be a Christian said, "It is not possible for me to hate anyone." Yet her conduct had all the elements of hatred. She left the church, and today she promotes all kinds of immoral conduct.

    If that woman had been perfectly frank with God and His people, she would have learned that good relationships depend on perfect love. "Perfect love casteth out fear" (1 John 4:18), even the fear of exposing our sins. Contrary to natural thinking, God loves us when we expose our badness to Him and ask Him to make us good. This truth comes to us from the story of the prodigal son in Luke 15. The wasted man went back to his father with nothing to recommend him. The father received him mercifully.

The Bible tells of many who enjoyed good relationships with God. Consider Joseph, for instance. His good relationship with others sprang out of a good relationship with God. He resisted the temptations of an ungodly woman, saying, "How . . . can I do this great wickedness, and sin against God?" (Genesis 39:9). He forgave his brothers and said, "God meant it unto good" (Genesis 50:20). Many other Bible stories record how the godly, because of their relationship with God, related properly to others. Others show how the ungodly, because they had no relationship with God, failed to relate properly to others.

The lesson for us is clear. When we believe that God loved us enough to send Jesus as the propitiation for our sins, we freely confess our sins and know that they are forgiven. Once our own relationship with the Lord is right, we become willing to freely forgive others who sin against us. We have the basis for good relationships with everyone.

*Chapter Two*

## *Relationships Within the Family*

The family is the foundation of all societal structures. Nations rise or fall according to the strength of their families. Where people keep marital commitments, and love and train their children, the nation has a foundation on which to build. This makes the maintenance of families of monumental importance. Lifestyles that alter traditional, Biblical marriage and family commitments, pave the way for colossal disaster.

Political men today talk about family values. It sounds good, but who in western culture knows what family values are? The erosion of family values has been going on for years. Few know anymore what they should expect from a family.

Family values involve relationships—husbands and wives to each other, children to parents, grandparents to their offspring, and children to children. In this chapter we want to consider how Christians should relate to each other in the family.

### A. Adults to Their Parents

When we marry, we leave our parents and establish another home. This is according to God's command. "For this cause shall a man leave his father and mother, and cleave to his wife" (Mark 10:7). This does not

*Relationships That Bless*

mean that grown children have no further obligation to their parents. The command "Honour thy father and mother" follows us through life, even when we no longer consult much with them about our decisions.

Jesus called the Jews of His day into question for trying to slip past the commandment to honor their parents. They had stipulated that if a man observed a certain legal technicality, he had no obligation to his parents. Jesus declared, "And ye suffer him no more to do ought for his father or his mother; making the word of God of none effect through your tradition" (Mark 7:10–13). *Honor* means "honor," and no word games can change that.

Nevertheless, followers of Jesus often face family conflicts. How can we live under the lordship of Jesus *and* in obedience to our parents? Not everyone can. Jesus said that His lordship would sometimes cause division in families. "A man's foes shall be they of his own household" (Matthew 10:36). Those foes could include parents.

If parents ask us to do things that we know God does not want us to do, we must obey God. But we must still honor our parents. Honor, after all, begins in our hearts. It shows in how we treat them and by the way we talk to them and about them.

I grew up in a church community where certain details of separation from the world were considered important. After we married, we moved to a distant community that observed different details of separation. My mother had been widowed at a young age, and she had carefully taught her family the way she knew our father would have taught us. This teaching included careful obedience to the standards of the church. As I considered the changes I would need to make to be conformed to the new church community, I thought about my mother. How would she feel about some changes I thought I should make? I wrote to her about the matter. Her reply indicated that she preferred that I continue the practices of my childhood teaching. However, at a later time when I was able to talk to her personally, she said, "You do what the Lord wants you to do." The very fact that I had discussed the matter with her was an honor to her. I could have reasoned that I had my own life to live, that I was following Jesus, and what my mother thought made no difference. But my mother *was* a godly woman.

I had made some changes to conform to the local church before I received approval from my mother. I made the changes because I knew that was what the Lord wanted me to do. I never despised my mother for what she thought. I never questioned the sincerity of her thinking. When we had an opportunity to discuss the matter together, there was complete respect and accord between us.

Even when this kind of accord is not possible, respect can be maintained in our hearts. That respect is translated into real deeds of kindness—not superficial niceties like giving expensive flowers on Mother's Day or cards with gushy messages. Parents usually are not fooled. They know what honor is.

Sometimes rebellious people take refuge in the words of Jesus: "A man's foes shall be they of his own household" (Matthew 10:36). Their rebellion is evident in the arrogant way they use this verse. They despise what their parents have taught them.

Some of their arguments might be true. Perhaps the traditions they were taught had become too traditional. Perhaps their parents were carnal in their efforts to get their ideas across. But it is still not right to despise what they taught, especially if they were serious in trying to do right.

Did not Jesus speak of hating parents? Yes, but in that context He spoke of hating our own life also (Luke 14:26). Followers of Jesus crucify themselves, not others. They are humble. They seek ways to show the love of Jesus. They are respectful and helpful to their parents wherever and whenever possible.

If we want our children to grow up to respect us, they must see us respecting our parents. "Rebuke not an elder, but intreat him as a father" (1 Timothy 5:1). We have excellent opportunities to show this respect when visiting our parents. If our children see us making sure our parents get the best chair, or adjusting a window shade to keep the sun from their eyes, they take note of it. If, when traveling, we take Miller Road instead of Mason Road because Father suggested it, that also shows respect.

Things become a bit more difficult if an aged parent lives with us and has decided opinions about how to fix the roof, cure an earache, entertain company, or discipline children. In the final analysis, we, and not our parents, are accountable to God for our household. With that accountability, God has given us authority. We must make our own choices.

Still, respect must not go out the window. We should smile and do it Grandma's way as a favor when we can, and teach our children to do the same. We might discover that she is wiser than we thought. If we must do differently than what she suggested, we should do it discreetly, or frankly explain why we are doing what we do.

Too often the picture is quite different from this. The problem is not the parent at all, but the young person who is eager to cast off the old restraints. Some of us might find it very much against our nature to have our parents telling us what to do. It should not be that way. If we have learned well what our parents have taught us, they will not be telling us what to do. We will be doing what they taught us.

Failing in this, we only fool ourselves. If we think we are now our own boss and quietly ignore the principles our parents have taught us, we are not independent. We only let someone other than our parents tell us what to do.

In the process, we strain the relationship with our parents. They may not say a thing about our violating what they taught, but our own conscience pricks us, and we imagine that our parents do not like us the way they used to. Isaiah explains how this works. "*Your* iniquities have separated between you and your God, and *your* sins have hid his face from you" (Isaiah 59:2).

The trend toward putting old people collectively in homes built just for them does not seem like the Christian thing to do. Where is the Biblical precedent for it? As much as they can, children should make it possible for their parents to live with them when they need care in their last years. I remember with pleasure how my mother took care of her parents in their last years. I am glad she also had daughters who took care of her. Thankfully, many today *are* caring for their parents in their declining years.

## Relationships Within the Family

God commanded Israel, "Thou shalt rise up before the hoary head, and honour the face of the old man, and fear thy God: I am the LORD" (Leviticus 19:32). In the Dominican Republic, out in the hill country, children bow respectfully to their elders. The elders often lay their hands on a child's head and pronounce a blessing on him. Does that not speak of a good relationship? Was there ever anything like that in North America? Is it one of those values that were lost many generations ago?

We can be respectful without being formal. We can cultivate good relationships without ceremonies. But to be totally unceremonious is not good either. Just as we have ordinances in church to keep valuable principles alive, our families should have some understandings too. Our parents will treasure the considerations they can count on from us.

## B. Husband to Wife

*1. The Standard*

"Husbands, love your wives, even as Christ also loved the church, and gave himself for it" (Ephesians 5:25). "Even as Christ also loved the church" puts every Christian husband under heavy obligation. How can any man love as Christ loved? Probably some newly wedded husbands think, "That will be no problem." Ere long they discover that they have in their heart a big lump of selfishness that makes it impossible to love as Christ loved.

Thankfully, for every impossibility that man confronts, God gives grace. With that grace, every Christian husband can develop a relationship with his wife that surpasses anything the world can know. This is not to say that unbelievers cannot enjoy a good marriage. Probably some do. But the Christian dimension makes a significant difference.

Another aspect of relating to our wives is found in the phrase "and gave himself for it." This speaks of what Christ did for the church. It was love that took Him through Gethsemane to Calvary. This same love can make a husband sacrifice and suffer for his wife. He gives his time—time that he thinks he cannot afford to give. He gives his energies to serve his wife—energies he would rather use on himself.

Why should a husband give himself for his wife? Is that not getting things backward? Is not the wife intended to be man's helper? Is not the man the head—the leader? Should not the wife give herself for her husband? Should she not always bend to his wishes? Should she not wait on her husband hand and foot? We can take a look at the life of Jesus for answers to these questions.

Jesus said of Himself, "For even the Son of man came not to be ministered unto, but to minister, and to give his life a ransom for many" (Mark 10:45). Jesus washed the disciples' feet; He was a living sacrifice. He lived to give, continually being helpful to someone. The husband who discovers the joy of doing things for his wife will no doubt have a wife who responds to him somewhat the same way the church responds to Christ.

The apostle Paul said, "But he that is married careth for the things of the world, how he may please his wife" (1 Corinthians 7:33). He considered marriage a hindrance to serving the Lord. He did not say it is wrong to marry. But he did indicate that a married man must take time to take care of his wife. It is not right for him to neglect his wife to serve the Lord in some other field. The Christian man learns to serve the Lord as he serves his wife.

This is natural when we remember that Christian husbands and wives are "heirs *together* of the grace of life" (1 Peter 3:7). They are both serving the Lord in their marriage. They are partners in their decisions about where and how they will serve the Lord. For example, they must have a satisfactory agreement on which church they will be a part of. The husband must be the leader, but he will give careful consideration to what his wife thinks on matters that affect their service to God.

If the Lord calls the husband to the ministry, the wife must accept this as a call from God to serve as a minister's wife. But the minister must not forget that he is the husband of the preacher's wife! It is not uncommon for a Christian minister to throw himself into his ministry and neglect his wife and family. Ministers should be considerate of their wives and be sure they are not overtaxed.

## Relationships Within the Family

Husbands, especially ministers, need to learn to know their wives. Peter directs us to "dwell with them according to knowledge" (1 Peter 3:7). What are your wife's strengths and weaknesses? What are the limits to which she can go? What are the signs of too much stress? Every woman is different. Do we know our wives well enough to take proper care of them?

Many times, if there is a strained relationship, it is not big things that make a difference. If your wife is showing signs of distress, do not ignore it. Helping her may only take an hour or two of sympathetic listening. One brother said that sometimes when his wife told him of a problem and he was trying to figure out a solution, she would say, "I'm not telling you because I want you to find an answer. I just want you to understand."

In a crisis, give your wife your full attention for however long it takes. Change schedules; cancel appointments; take off work if need be. She needs to know that she is the most important person in your life. If you have neglected to keep her assured of her importance to you, you will want to take special measures to restore that assurance in her heart.

Then stay sensitive to her needs. Take her for a walk in the woods. Take her shopping. Spend time with her in the garden. Share with her in whatever you know she enjoys. The fact that you are willing to sometimes change your schedule to give her your time and attention can make a great difference.

Sometimes we forget how it is for women. Most men derive satisfaction from a great variety of relationships outside the home. We feel useful and needed as we help others. Since we are useful to others, we feel secure. From where do our wives derive their sense of importance?

She gets it from her family, of course. But it must be from more than the children. If the husband always thinks of his wife as the most important person in his life (next to God, that is) he will treat her as such. She will be content, happy, and secure. But with all his other involvements, a man can without thinking neglect his relationship with his wife. For this reason, after six to ten years of marriage, a husband needs to consider his relationship with his wife. Has it fallen into a meaningless routine? Is he sure that his wife is completely satisfied with him?

In case we still have difficulty understanding the extent of Christ's love for the church, the Bible gives us another standard that we can understand. "So ought men to love their wives as their own bodies" (Ephesians 5:28). We know how much we love our own bodies. When our wives are tired or have a headache, the Lord expects us to be as sympathetic with them as we are with ourselves. To translate that love for ourselves into love for our wives requires special grace and self-denial. But if we obey this command, it pays great dividends.

2. *"Due Benevolence"*

"Let the husband render unto the wife due benevolence: and likewise also the wife unto the husband" (1 Corinthians 7:3).

Benevolence speaks of generosity. A wife responds well to tenderness and thoughtfulness. Note the effort your wife puts into making clothes for the family. If she is artistic in the way she designs a meal, commend her for it. If she has risked putting your desk in order, do not complain that you cannot find what you are looking for. You could not have found it otherwise either. If you pleasantly ask her, she may direct you right to it.

The man who grows in appreciation and admiration for his wife for the first fifteen years of their marriage will usually continue to do so for the rest of his life. But relationships will deteriorate if he fails to maintain a benevolent disposition.

Husbands need to exercise special benevolence during those stressful times before and after childbirth. The mother needs all the rest she can get. She must devote time and attention to the baby. The other children need attention. People are coming and going. Schedules are hard to maintain. At such a time, the Christian husband will do all he can to make the home chores go smoothly. Rather than making demands of his wife, he will make demands of himself. He will fulfill his promise to "love and cherish her, provide and care for her in health and in sickness, in prosperity and in adversity."

## 3. The Husband's Marital Powers

"The wife hath not power over her own body, but the husband: and likewise also the husband hath not power of his own body, but the wife" (1 Corinthians 7:4).

In focus is the way the husband and wife give themselves to each other in the marriage union and the power they exercise over each other in that relationship.

God made men and women feel attracted to each other. We carry desires that bring us together in marriage. God designed our desires to be satisfied and sanctified in the marriage union. Although the desires of the husband and those of his wife are not exactly the same, they both can be perfectly fulfilled.

However, the difference in the dispositions of a husband and a wife requires each to practice self-denial. Some women have a great need for amorous attention that their mate can hardly supply. A wife of this disposition must learn by God's grace to deny herself and be happy with what her husband does give. Some men desire more intimacy than their wives can sustain. Such husbands must by God's grace deny themselves and believe that God gave them a mate suitable for them. This is where divine grace makes the Christian marriage far superior to secular marriage. Where both husband and wife have learned to practice unselfish love, the marriage union proves to be a great blessing. But if either one becomes selfish, the blessings quickly diminish.

The power that marriage partners exercise over each other is both an opportunity and a responsibility? In marriage, two become one. They are no longer their own. Some married people think of their union as an opportunity for personal gratification, only to become bored or even disgusted. Rather, each married partner has the opportunity and responsibility to please the other, and in so doing finds his own needs met.

The marriage union is profound. It provides both husband and wife with sanctified pleasures that penetrate beyond the superficial or obvious. The emotional union is even more important than the physical one. The husband or wife can partake of the emotions of the other, or refuse to do so. Each can abuse his power over the other, or can use that power to be complementary and supportive.

Since much of marriage is private, God alone knows how often this power is misused. But it cannot be misused without damaging relationships. An unfulfilled wife cannot hide her sadness. Neither can a distraught husband hide his problem. When a marriage fails to provide God-designed fulfillment, it is right to seek help from someone you can trust. The world's marriage counselors are generally not safe, but by asking a few questions you can find someone who is both competent and spiritual.

*4. Defraud Not*

"Defraud ye not one the other, except it be with consent for a time, that ye may give yourselves to fasting and prayer; and come together again, that Satan tempt you not for your incontinency" (1 Corinthians 7:5).

*Defraud* means "to take something by fraud; swindle." Can this happen between marriage partners?

The word *defraud* is used in the context of the powers that married partners have with one another's body. The physical union is one powerful element in the bonding aspect of marriage. Because of its profound effect, a person can abuse this power to defraud his partner. If a husband is disappointed in his wife's performance, he may defraud his wife of the benevolence due her. If a wife begins to feel that she is not respected, or that her husband is not the loving man she married, she may defraud her husband of the benevolence due him. This creates a stressful relationship that keeps a marriage from functioning as God planned, until there is confession and repentance. "Let not the sun go down upon your wrath" certainly applies here.

The Christian husband relates to his wife according to the direction that God gives in His Word rather than according to what he may think his wife deserves. A husband never has the right to decide whether his wife is worthy of his love and attentions. He has promised to love, cherish, care for, and provide for his wife. He must fulfill that promise regardless of his wife's response. Of course he hopes she will respond in love, but he keeps his promise to God even if she does not.

Marriage is based on commitment, not on love. Of course love is what brings people together to the marriage union. But people are not married until they make a covenant that binds them together for life. After the covenant is made, it forms the basis for the love. There is no place for fraud in this relationship.

Life often brings us experiences that test our commitment to love. In a disappointing experience, we can withhold ourselves from the other person, or we can forgive. Paul's injunction comes into focus here. "Husbands, love your wives, and be not bitter against them" (Colossians 3:19). Those who do not forgive turn bitter. Everything that happens from that point on, they interpret from the context of a bitter heart. As a result, the relationship turns from bliss to bondage. If husband and wife had refused to cheat each other of forgiveness and love, they would have never defrauded each other in actual deed.

5. *Harmony and Disharmony in Marriage*

"Likewise, ye husbands, dwell with them according to knowledge, giving honour unto the wife, as unto the weaker vessel, and as being heirs together of the grace of life; that your prayers be not hindered" (1 Peter 3:7).

Harmonious marital relationships affect our relationship with God. So do unharmonious relationships. Peter indicates here that we cannot pray well if we do not have a good relationship with our wives. This stands to reason. Besides affecting our friendship with the Lord, a bad marital relationship will dominate the mind. We cannot pray freely if we have a bad relationship to deal with every day.

Sometimes we are tempted to think that if we ignore a problem, it will go away. It does not work that way. It is like a bad debt; it accumulates interest that no one will pay. We must face difficult situations like men. This includes the husband honoring his wife, understanding that she is the weaker vessel, and remembering that she is a fellow heir of the grace of life. It also includes fasting and prayer, beseeching God to help us through our difficulties.

We husbands will find solutions to problems more rapidly if we consider ourselves to be the major part of any difficulty. We have more control over our ways than we do over the ways of our wives. If we do something that causes stress for our wives, why not apologize? This is such a simple act, yet it is important for continuous marital harmony. Far too many people are too proud to admit failure. If a man is too proud to say, "I'm sorry," he cannot relate properly to his wife.

If your wife is doing something that irks you, live with it for a while and pray much about the matter. Is it something she can change? Has your relationship developed to the point that your wife has no reason to doubt that she is the best woman in the world to you? Or is she someone who battles feelings of insecurity? After some prayerful consideration, you may decide to love the very thing that irked you because it is a part of your wife.

On the other hand, you may decide that she would want you to share with her how you feel about the matter. If you humbly admit that probably there are areas in your own life more objectionable than what you are mentioning, it will help to put her at ease. Make it appear as small as it likely is. Perhaps mention it only in passing. A formal introduction, buildup, climax, and conclusion might be just too much. If you give "honour unto the wife, as unto the weaker vessel, and as being heirs together of the grace of life," your wife will see and feel that you really love and care about her. You may even want to assure her that if it is something she cannot change or is something that may take some time to change, you will gladly be considerate.

A typical Christian wife generally will not resent being asked to change something about her housekeeping or habits. She wants to please her husband because that is part of making a happy home. Yet a husband must be careful not to tread on sensitive feelings. If a wife gets hurt too often, she will develop emotional calluses that help deaden her pain. But those same calluses will also start to deaden something in her spirit—shall we call it girlishness? Whatever it is, nearly any husband treasures it and would regret the loss if it were gone.

If your wife is one who cannot freely admit failure, you will want to be forgiving and pray much that God would do His work of grace in her heart. Do not try to change your wife's spirit. You cannot. You will probably make matters worse and only increase her fears. Commit the matter to God. He can make needed changes in your heart as well as in the heart of your wife.

## 6. Handling Our Feelings

What makes us feel the way we do? Why do we love some people more than others? What causes a husband's love for his wife to change? Careful self-analysis reveals that our natural love for others is based on how they treat us. Jesus dealt with this problem. "For if ye love them which love you, what reward have ye? do not even the publicans the same?" (Matthew 5:46).

Jesus was calling us to rise above this, to deal with people on a higher level than we think they have dealt with us. When we become irritated by something our wives do, we need not respond in irritation. We can talk to God until the irritation is gone.

It is important not to confront a matter while we are irked about it because we will make the matter bigger than it is. We might add items to our statements that we did not intend to say. This could shake our wife's confidence in us.

If this ever happens to you, do not let the sun go down before you repent. Confess your sin to your wife privately (publicly if the children heard you), and do something special for her to prove that you are truly repentant. Confession of sin is one of the marvelous options God has given us. Through repentance and forgiveness, we failing humans can maintain valuable relationships.

Whatever we do, let us not let feelings reign.

## 7. The Reticent Husband With a Dominant Wife

A reticent husband is quiet by nature. He would rather keep his thoughts to himself than share them. Since he finds it hard to express his ideas, he would rather listen. Frequently, a man of this nature will marry a woman with a dominant nature. If the wife is the more aggressive of the two, how can the husband be the leader as the Bible commands?

## Relationships That Bless

We need not try to change our personalities. God gives them to us. He makes some men quiet and retiring by nature. He makes some women naturally confident and enterprising.

At the same time, it is not right just to follow our nature. Should the husband let the wife go ahead since she naturally is a leader? If he does, he is headed for trouble. The reticent husband will need to ask God to help him take responsibility for the direction of the home. If his wife is quick-witted and wise, he should benefit from her wisdom. If his wife is dominant but not wise, he will need wisdom to show her that her thinking is not sound.

How he does this is important. He must not try to make her look foolish. He may say, "It sounds like a good idea, but . . ." There are ways of showing a person his error in thinking and still maintaining that person's dignity.

Larry was a reticent young man. He found himself attracted to Sarah, an aggressive young lady. When he started courting her, many shook their heads in disbelief. Such a marriage would only yield problems. No doubt some of the gossip filtered back to Larry. He was no carnal young man, and he realized the potential problems in marrying her. Being a man of God, he found a way through. After praying about it, he decided to handle the matter with complete candor. "Sarah, I'd like to ask you to be my wife, but I must know something first. You are quite forward and outspoken, and I am quite the opposite. If you were my wife, could you promise to always let me be the leader?" After careful consideration, she promised. The marriage blossomed into a gracious union.

Married couples who are yielded to Christ can help each other much. Those who are very different from each other can work together harmoniously when they discover the great value of their partner's contribution. The quiet husband can be a quiet leader. He need not take an adversarial stance, always critically reviewing his wife's proposals and saying no sometimes just as a matter of policy. On the other hand, if at any point he begins to let his wife have her way simply because it goes more smoothly that way, the marriage will deteriorate.

8. *Relating to Your Wife on Money Matters*

Financial matters can be a source of conflict in marriage. Some people are very tight and saving. Some are careful but willing to share. Others simply spend all they make. And today many spend more than they make.

Obviously, the ability to manage money varies greatly. God did not make all men wiser than women in money management. Some women are quite gifted in this field. Proverbs 31 portrays the virtuous woman involved in financial matters. If your wife has superior insights in money management, thank God for her insight. Allow it to bless the union.

On the other hand, if your wife spends money too freely, consider the matter carefully. You could decide to handle all money matters yourself. But most wives would interpret that as a breach of trust. It is better to sit down and frankly talk it over with your wife. Establish some guidelines together. Then trust her.

Most husbands make mistakes in money matters, whether they like to admit it or not. If your wife spends money that you think she should not have, do not act too wise. Ask her why she made the purchase. Maybe her reasoning makes sense. If it does, say so. If it does not, ask more questions. If she fails to convince you, admit that you do not always spend money wisely either.

Sometimes you may need to discuss a money matter extensively in order to understand each other. But make disposition of the matter in such a way that there is no continuing conflict. Money is not important enough to allow it to cause continuing conflict in your marriage.

9. *Respecting Your Wife as a Person*

Husbands who want good relationships with their wives will respect them as persons with feelings, opinions, rights and convictions. Instead of trying to destroy their individuality or trying to subjugate them, they will allow them to exercise their abilities in a way that benefits the union.

Men who feel insecure in their relationship to God tend to become fearful of a spiritual wife. This state of affairs they can and must change.

A husband should be glad if his wife is wiser than he. A foolish husband will become fearful and deny the wisdom of his wife and may even poke fun at what she thinks. You can guess what happens to the relationship.

Husband, learn to know your wife. Dwell with her according to that knowledge. Compliment your wife for the good things she adds to the union. This will feed the flame of love in your heart and in hers. Your wife will be a secure woman. In that security you will be able to share without fear the deep secrets of your hearts.

"Husbands, love your wives, even as Christ also loved the church, and gave himself for it. . . . So ought men to love their wives as their own bodies. He that loveth his wife loveth himself" (Ephesians 5:25–29).

## C. Wife to Husband

"Wives, submit yourselves unto your own husbands, as unto the Lord. For the husband is the head of the wife, even as Christ is the head of the church: and he is the saviour of the body. Therefore as the church is subject unto Christ, so let the wives be to their own husbands in every thing" (Ephesians 5:22–25).

"And the wife see that she reverence her husband" (Ephesians 5:33).

*1. Submission and Reverence*

We see from the above verses that the wife's contribution to a good marital relationship lies basically in two attitudes—submission and reverence. These two attitudes are very closely tied together. We will gladly submit to someone we reverence. Any failure to fulfill God's requirement in either of these attitudes will affect the other too.

How can a wife submit to and reverence someone who is less than perfect? Again, the above verses give the answer. A wife is to relate to her husband "as unto the Lord." She is to obey her husband—yes, cheerfully—by focusing on obedience to Christ and His commands.

Subjection to a husband in everything as the Bible commands may seem risky to a new bride. It is. Marriage is venturesome for all of us. The normal desire for companionship and the love we have for each other urge us to take the risk, promising that love will solve most of our problems. The experiences of life soon force us to face reality. Our love is not so intense and all encompassing as we thought. What we thought was a powerful element in our life turns out to be only a little seed that must finish germinating before it can begin to grow and mature. Selfishness, which we thought was so far removed from this relationship, is after all very close to the surface.

As time goes on, however, something happens that we were perhaps not expecting. Marital love goes through test after test. As we pass each test, our love grows stronger. It matures with age and becomes the powerful element that we envisioned at the beginning.

Our relationship with the Lord grows too. You, wife, will learn that each time you submit to your husband, God smiles upon you. This is especially true if the submission has been difficult. Nothing is more important in the life of a Christian woman than to know that God approves of her life.

A wife may be able in her own mind to justify a point of insubordination, but that will not take the weight of guilt from her heart. The Scriptures stand: "Therefore as the church is subject unto Christ, so let the wives be to their own husbands in every thing." Hopefully you have a Christian husband. But even if you do not, obedience to Christ in this matter will bring you God's reward of blessing and peace.

The marital relationship is reciprocal. That is, it depends on input from two sides. It means giving and receiving, with both sides giving and both receiving. Generally, the more we give, the more we receive. Wife, if you discover the joy of giving without watching for returns, you will have peace and joy in abundance. When you begin to compare the returns with what you give, you are being selfish. You will not even be able to appreciate all that you do get. Selfishness will blind your eyes. But if you can learn from Jesus' example to be sacrificial, you will be blessed. The poet wrote, "I would be giving and forget the gift." That is where real blessings flow.

By nature women tend to be more sacrificial than men. The Bible records how various women ministered to Jesus. "There were also women looking on afar off: among whom was Mary Magdalene, and Mary the mother of James the less and of Joses, and Salome; (who also, when he was in Galilee, followed him, and ministered unto him;) and many other women which came up with him unto Jerusalem" (Mark 15:40, 41). Paul in his epistles also gave recognition to the services of many women.

Every Christian wife who faithfully fills her place in the home will be highly honored in this life and in the life to come. When you need inspiration, read Proverbs 31 and note the glorious position a wife holds. "Her children arise up, and call her blessed; her husband also, and he praiseth her" (verse 28). To the wife who does not enjoy a good marital relationship, Proverbs 31 is a mockery.

Sometimes a wife sees her husband as the real problem. She thinks he has failed to give her due Biblical respect. If your marriage is lacking, rather than focusing on your husband's failure, look within your own heart for ways in which you could change. Maybe you are not the virtuous woman you think you are. Maybe you have room to improve. Concentrate on that for a while. If you change your attitude, you might discover that your husband has changed too.

Consider the options God gives you in your submissive role. Study your husband's likes and dislikes. Think of ways to gain his respect. Ask God to give you a forgiving heart. Ask Him to remove from your mind those things that make it difficult to reverence your husband.

The husband who knows that his wife is trying to please him will usually respond in kindness and consideration. There may be exceptions, but do not be quick to say that your husband is an exception. Regardless of your husband's conduct, you can benefit from being Christlike in all you do. When you live as unto the Lord, you will have abundant peace and power.

Since you are probably a sacrificial wife by nature, you can use that ability to serve your husband in a way that will bring great returns. Dote over your husband, with discretion, of course, but sincerely. Make him feel that he is the most important man in your life. Show appreciation for everything he does, and hopefully he will do more for you to maintain your affection. As love and affection flow back and forth, you will be experiencing the blessings God intended.

Do not be dismayed if you feel one day that he failed to reciprocate as you expected. Pour on more affection and pray for him. He may need a nudge in the right direction at times. But do it lovingly. Do not nag.

Since few men are naturally sacrificial, they do not always see where they could be more helpful. Even when they do see it, they might take some time before they actually offer help. They might even wait until they are asked. A wife needs patience and grace not to become resentful about this. How can a wife reverence a husband who needs to be asked for help?

It is a choice you make. You can resent his thoughtlessness, or you can admire and reverence him for the qualities he does have. Consider what makes him special to you. What attracted you to your husband in the first place? Do those qualities still exist? If you continually reverence your husband, he will more easily respect you. If you begin to despise him, he will know it, and the relationship will suffer.

Keep the lines of communication open. If you need help, ask him for help. If he helps you, thank him. If he does not, pray for him, and pray for yourself. God can do more in his heart than you can. If you pray for him because you really love him, God will give you wisdom and grace to know how to handle matters as they arise.

If you have a Christian husband, you should be able to confront him on any matter. Make sure your heart is free from bitterness, or bitterness will filter into what you say. If, however, you cannot free your heart of its resentment, tell him the situation as it is. Tell him, "I need help." Tell him that you are fighting resentment, and you are not winning the battle. Explain what the resentment is about. Own it as your problem but enlist his help. Since your resentment is toward him, he must be part of the solution. Do not be too proud to admit your need. There is nothing debasing about owning our need. It will help solve the problem.

Some women have much greater physical and emotional stamina than others. If you have difficulty taking care of four preschool children without help, say so. Your husband may be able to give the extra help, or he may help you find some other way to take care of the need. If you can take care of the household duties with time to spare, you may want to help your husband in his work. The important thing is for both you and your husband to be happy with the arrangement.

*2. The Wife's Marital Powers*

"The wife hath not power of her own body, but the husband: and likewise also the husband hath not power of his own body, but the wife. Defraud ye not one the other" (1 Corinthians 7:4, 5).

Anyone can misuse power. You may be tempted, under certain circumstances, to misuse the power described here by withholding yourself from your husband. It may be retaliation—since your husband misused his power, you feel justified in misusing yours. You cannot do this and be free before God.

Use your powers for good. God created man with desires that can become a temptation if he cannot enjoy a good marital relationship. But if a woman relates lovingly to her husband, she not only reduces his temptations but also helps to build a secure home for herself.

The only reason that Paul gives for refraining from each other is for prayer and fasting. He speaks of it being "with consent." This means that the abstinence is agreed upon.

Duties of motherhood can make a wife feel that she cannot give her husband all the attention he desires. Both husbands and wives must be especially considerate in times of stress. Talk it over. Consider options that will give you the needed time and energy to perform your responsibilities.

You as a wife may need to initiate the discussion. You may think that it is the husband's duty to initiate any discussion on such matters, but you may do it. Your husband may not even be aware of the turmoil in your mind. Being submissive does not mean that you cannot talk to him. It does not mean that you cannot question the justice of what he expects of you. But the questions need to be in the open and be discussed.

In any discussion, try to see matters from your husband's perspective as well as from your own. As you try to understand your husband, hopefully he will try to understand you. Talk to God together about the matter and seek His wisdom. God has promised to give wisdom liberally to those who ask.

If your husband feels inferior, assure him of your love. Tell him what you appreciate about him. If you need to question him, let him know that you are only raising questions to be helpful.

Be sure, of course, that this is true. Some insecure women try to belittle their husbands to boost their own ego. This destroys relationships.

*3. Shattered Dreams*

How does a wife handle shattered dreams? Should she never have dreamed them in the first place? The value of dreams could be questioned, but they seem to be a fact of youthful lives. Young people like to think that living with one they love will bring them bliss. It does, but not without trials. That wonderful, considerate young man begins to show another side of himself. He is not the unselfish man we envisioned. How can he be so thoughtless? Why does he act as he does now?

One mother, in trying to prepare her daughter for marriage, said, "Remember, you marry a sinner." No doubt she was overstating her point because sinners can be saved by the grace of God. She probably meant that no man is ever sanctified to the point that you can no longer see imperfections in him. You can focus on the bad in him, or you can consider his value.

Dreams are idealistic. They present a danger to us since they are not realistic. Some people think the only way to keep a relationship intact is to keep the dreams intact. Actually, facing reality need not destroy a relationship. Rather, it strengthens the relationship. When you discover that your husband is a failing human just like yourself, it should put you at ease in his presence. His failures are no reason to despise or belittle him. Instead, you should admire the strength of character he possesses in spite of his humanness.

Ideals have their benefits. Someone without ideals will be a drifter. Ideals are goals toward which we move. We need to know what kind of relationship we want so that we can work toward achieving it. What do you need to do to bring about the closeness you believe to be ideal?

Does the success of that ideal lie mostly in your husband's hands? If you as a wife concentrate on your own input, you will likely realize your goal much sooner than if you concentrate on your husband's part. You will bring out the best in your husband as you put your best into the union.

*4. The Dominant Wife With a Reticent Husband*

It is not right for the dominant wife simply to follow her nature. For you to be a Christian wife, your nature must be brought under the control of divine grace. If your husband is reticent by nature, you might easily take advantage of him. Learn not to express your opinion about a matter too quickly. Give your husband time to think things through. Learn not to feel too strongly about your opinions. No matter how capable you may be, it is not right for you to usurp authority over your husband (1 Timothy 2:11, 12).

Carol was a strong-natured, talented woman with a Christian upbringing. Her husband, Theodore, was a capable and intelligent man. But he tended to doubt his own abilities and sometimes withdrew when he should have moved ahead. Carol occasionally made matters worse for him by contesting his decisions (which admittedly were not always the wisest). As time went on, the two of them slipped subconsciously into a strong-weak relationship, with Carol being the strong one and Theodore taking a secondary role.

Theodore kept withdrawing, not only from Carol, but from his work and from the church. Carol was not really happy with the state of affairs, even when she got her own way. Finally she sought help from a friend.

The friend said, "Never underestimate the power of helplessness. Babies left on doorsteps are always taken care of." That fit with what Carol had already noticed. When she had had a hospital experience and was relatively helpless, Theodore had risen to the challenge.

The friend also said, "In order for one partner to be a weak one, there has to be a strong one." Carol would need to shift from a strong stance to a weak one to encourage her husband to fill his proper role. She would need to leave the driver's seat empty. She would no longer do things for

Theodore and be upset because she had to do them, but simply wait on him to do them.

Carol never did completely master this, partly because Theodore never completely mastered his part. But as time went on, their marriage became somewhat more comfortable, especially when Theodore was fulfilling a man's role.

The dominant wife must learn to wait. If you keep quiet until your husband has had time to speak, you may discover that he does some good thinking. If he discovers that you are quick-witted and usually wise in your evaluations, he may want you to present your views before he even begins to think about it. This might be all right, but you must insist that your husband make the final decision. You will want to know that your husband indeed believes your idea is the right way to go, and has not consented only because he knows you will be unhappy if he does not.

Some men battle inferior feelings when their wives seem wiser than they. Often such men will not give their wives the personal freedom that is rightfully theirs. They may interpret many things as an infringement on their authority. If your husband is like this, you can become resentful, or you can try to see things from his perspective. Defer to him with a smile at every opportunity. This should allay his fear that you are trying to be the leader.

Freely commend your husband for his good qualities. Direct compliments might have a place, but the best are the ones he overhears. One compliment you might have overlooked is the simple "I'll talk to my husband about that and get back with you after we decide." Under such genial treatment, he may gradually develop the sense of security that he needs.

The woman who flaunts her abilities is not reverencing her husband. She is not seeking a good relationship. It is a selfish, carnal, sinful satisfaction to glory in the fact that we are superior to another. Some women frequently say, "I told John this" and "I told John that." This might be perfectly innocent and indicate that they are communicating well. On the other hand, it might indicate who is leading. Women have the right and responsibility to tell their husbands things. Their insights are valuable, but they are not to be publicly brandished.

How important is a good relationship with your husband? It is second only to your relationship with God. Concentrate on what you can do to make that relationship the very best. Bring your powers under the influence of divine grace. Submit to your husband in everything and reverence him. You then will be a wife that he will want to love even as Christ loved the church. He will want to nourish and cherish you.

5. *Selfishness Destroys*

Remember that the great destroyer of relationships is selfishness. If your husband becomes selfish in a moment of weakness, do not respond with selfishness. Your kindness and unselfishness will reveal his weakness to him far more quickly than retaliation will. Consider the long-range effect of what you do. Be like Jesus, who accepted loss to win in the end, and you will be right.

Husbands and wives should see their marriage as a building project. God laid the foundation, and now they each add their little deeds to the building each day. Many times we need to consult the "blueprint" to see what is the right thing to do. When we rationalize about matters, we usually come to the wrong conclusions. But when we consider the will of God, He guides us to the right way.

As Paul states in 1 Corinthians 3:9–13, some build with gold, silver, and precious stones; others use wood, hay, and stubble. In home building, the difference between gold and straw is often the difference between selfishness and unselfishness.

6. *The Ungodly Husband*

Sometimes a Christian woman finds herself married to an ungodly husband for reasons which may or may not be her fault. At any rate, placing blame does not solve her main question, which is, "What shall I do now?"

A Christian woman normally should not seek separation from her husband (1 Corinthians 7:10, 13). If it seems impossible for her to stay

Relationships Within the Family

with her husband because she fears for her physical or moral safety, or that of her children, she needs to work closely with her church leaders to find a suitable solution. She should never decide on her own to walk out. If she is part of Scriptural church setting, a Christian wife of an ungodly husband has resources to draw from before she comes to this point. She should have a friend with whom to share her woes, who will pray for her and with her when the days are difficult. Not least, she should remember to pour out her heart to the Lord, who understands perfectly and sometimes will answer in ways she was not expecting.

In difficult situations, the Lord gives grace that often surprises onlookers. Visitors to the home of one woman in an abusive situation were impressed that her children did not speak disrespectfully of their father, in spite of his ungodly ways. This gave evidence that although life was thorny, their godly mother was finding a pathway.

## D. Parents to Children

"Lo, children are an heritage of the LORD: and the fruit of the womb is his reward. As arrows are in the hand of a mighty man; so are children of the youth. Happy is the man that hath his quiver full of them: they shall not be ashamed, but they shall speak with the enemies in the gate" (Psalm 127:3–5).

What do you think of your children? Do you see them as gifts from God? Is that eighth or tenth child another special reward from God? Is he as precious as the first one? Is he an immortal soul to be nourished for the Lord? Or is he simply a biological byproduct to you, another mouth to feed? How we view the child will make a world of difference in the way we relate to him.

*1. The Biblical View of Conception*

Every conception is an act of God. "My substance was not hid from thee, when I was made in secret, and curiously wrought in the lowest parts of the earth. Thine eyes did see my substance, yet being unperfect; and in thy book all my members were written, which in continuance were fashioned, when as yet there was none of them" (Psalm 139:15, 16). Parents who believe that conception is an act of God will reverence life and will relate to their child in a manner that God can bless.

Those who view their children mainly from a biological standpoint will not and cannot relate properly to them. They will resort to modern means of birth control that limit a family to two or three children. We are appalled at the number of so-called Christian counselors who freely promote this modern view of the family. From this cheap concept of human conception springs the problem of child abuse. When respect for a child is lacking from the very beginning, we may expect it to be lacking later as well. May God bring a revival of the Biblical view of the child.

True Christians love children and want families. This love provides a climate in which to train and nurture children. A little baby soon detects if he is wanted or not. He feels love in the way he is handled and cared for. We cannot think one way about him and communicate something else.

We never know what kind of child God will give us. We do hope and pray for a normal child. But sometimes God gives us a special child—one who is not normal and takes much extra care. Even among those we consider normal, we find a wide range of characteristics. One is of quick intelligence, and one is slow at learning. One is diligent by nature, and another is untidy. The diligent one will easily win our favor and the other our disfavor. This will affect relationships. Paul asked some questions that put this in perspective. "For who maketh thee to differ from another? and what hast thou that thou didst not receive? now if thou didst receive it, why dost thou glory, as if thou hadst not received it?" (1 Corinthians 4:7). Certainly, children become increasingly responsible for what they do with their tendencies, but they should not suffer from a parent's resentment of their inborn weaknesses. They need guidance and correction.

2. *Treating Children as Individuals*

All children have points of excellence as well as obvious weaknesses. We encourage them to overcome their weaknesses as much as possible, and we commend them for things they do well. We should help our children understand that talent does not make them better than others; it only makes them different. Since we are all different in some way, we want to be humble about our particular difference. The best way to be humble is to stop dwelling on how talented we are and go on to other interesting subjects.

The Christian home is the ideal place to teach this principle of accepting and benefiting each other. Parents must not let a gifted child flaunt his abilities. Neither must they let a less gifted child become sullen because of his own pride. Pride of whatever form damages character.

Parents need the wisdom of God as they confront relationship problems with children. But the Lord's promise is, "If any of you lack wisdom, let him ask of God, that giveth to all men liberally, and upbraideth not; and it shall be given him" (James 1:5). If we do not seek the wisdom of God, we will often be frustrated. If we maintain our faith, we will marvel again and again at how God enables us to do what is right. There is a solution to every difficulty.

Sometimes we may need to reach beyond ourselves and our home to find solutions. Parents need to be humble enough to admit needs. Church leaders can often help us. Another parent who has faced similar situations can be helpful. Parents often battle pride and do not realize that this is keeping them from asking advice. If we are not finding a solution to a problem, we should consider the possibility of pride in our hearts.

*3. The Father's Responsibility*

The Bible lays a heavy obligation upon every father. "And, ye fathers, provoke not your children to wrath: but bring them up in the nurture and admonition of the Lord" (Ephesians 6:4). Fathers can do things that anger their children. This happens mostly when the father is not consistent in what he requires or in how he disciplines.

A wife can help her husband see where he is inconsistent. This must be done in private. The Christian husband will then make the necessary amendments. If he does not see where he is wrong, his wife will need to pray further for her husband. If he still does not see his need to change his ways, she may need to seek help from a minister.

A woman might be tempted to get out of her place when her husband fails. But to openly oppose her husband will quickly destroy parental authority. Neither parent can afford that.

*4. Controlling the Workload*

Sometimes God gives Christians large families, and it requires diligence to care for them properly. Mothers and fathers both can become weary of the toil involved. In their efforts to provide for their children physically, they may neglect spiritual nurture.

The father and mother who regularly take time to read Bible stories to little ones will be rewarded with a relationship that both parents and children will value years later. Help them prepare for Sunday school. Join them in their memory assignments. Take an interest in their sandbox projects and domino towers to let them know you care about them. These little things help to build a relationship that will be even more important in adolescence.

Affluence has not aided us in child nurture. Many things have entered the home that destroy the interaction of the family. Computers, tapes, dishwashers—perhaps we can afford these things, monetarily. Many other things have been disappearing from the home: daily chores for children, gardening and canning, the need to "do without." Are parents still teaching their children the disciplines they will need in life? Is the business or the farm stealing precious family time? We cannot afford, spiritually, to neglect the nurture of eternal souls in favor of wealth.

Parents are in charge of how much work they do in a day. Some fathers think the whole family must be kept busy—children as well as parents. They do not know how to plan valuable leisure time for family benefit. This invariably maintains a tense atmosphere. At the other extreme are fathers who do not know how to keep the family properly occupied. Because of a high wage, they have abundance of leisure. They may spend their free time in recreations that do not develop meaningful relationships.

There are ways of building good parent–child relationships, but these ways require forethought. We have to consider what we want to teach.

We cannot do things the way the world does, or we will reap the same failures they reap.

5. *Guiding Youth*

Adolescence often presents a crisis in relationships. Many adolescents begin to question the values of their parents. Their reasoning powers are developing, and it is quite normal for them to evaluate things they have been taught. Parents learn at that point whether they have done their job well. If the parents have provided a stable, secure relationship up to this time, the child will very likely continue to accept the direction of his parents. If the relationship has not maintained the confidence of the child, he will be greatly troubled.

It is important for parents to be wise enough to turn to God if relationships are troubled. Parents may be tempted to use force if a youth becomes rebellious. Depending on the age and the nature of the child, this could make matters worse. Parents need to humble themselves and consider where they have failed. They need to confess their failures to God and to the child and pray that God would deal mercifully with the child to bring him to repentance. God can do things we cannot do. If parents are too proud to admit failure, problems will increase.

While admitting failure, however, we should not be afraid to draw clear lines. Our hands are not completely tied, and we should say no when necessary. God condemned Eli, an Old Testament priest, "because his sons made themselves vile, and he restrained them not" (1 Samuel 3:13).

Neither should we absolve a youth of his accountability. "Even a child is known by his doings, whether his work be pure, and whether it be right" (Proverbs 20:11). "Children, obey your parents in the Lord: for this is right. Honour thy father and mother; which is the first commandment with promise; that it may be well with thee, and thou mayest live long on the earth" (Ephesians 6:1–3).

These verses do not say a child should honor and obey parents only if the parents are good. Children do not appraise these matters very well. They must obey and honor their parents even though their parents might be failing in some ways.

## 6. *Mending Relationships*

Mending relationships requires much more effort than maintaining them. For that reason, it is important to pay attention to little things. Take time to play with the children. Read to them. Pray with them. Show interest in what they are doing.

Guard against always being negative to their ideas. As a parent, I found it easy to say no without considering at length why I said no. A busy parent might think that he does not have time to enter into a child's project. A father may think that he does not have the money to do something that his son wants him to do. If it is beneficial and helps to maintain a good relationship, it may be the best investment he could make.

Parents may not always be aware of a deteriorating relationship until it has gone far. Or they may think that the situation really is not too serious and that with time it will get better. This may be true, but it might also get worse. It may disappear for a while, only to emerge from the memory at the next provocation. After a while it can become a great big load that causes a relationship to break down. Mending such relationships will consume much more time than maintaining good relationships along the way.

## 7. *Relating to the Willful*

How can parents relate properly to a willful child—one who at a very young age deliberately does what he is told not to do? Some children carry a strong determination to do what *they* want to do. These children require much love and discipline. If the first child is very obedient and easy to train and the next one is the opposite, parents often do not know what to do. It is easy to love the first one and despise the next one. This aggravates the problem.

The willful child needs more love, not less. He also needs more discipline. A parent must also assure him that he is loved, though disciplined more. Actually, to an extent, the discipline itself can reassure him of that fact. One help in relating to this child is that a parent generally knows what the child is thinking.

Every child is different, and each one requires his own kind of attention. It is important to develop a meaningful relationship with each one. Sometimes one parent may find it easier than the other to relate to a certain child. This requires special understanding on the part of both parents. It is no reason to reflect on one another. Make sure that you agree as parents on what you want for your children. Then the parent who communicates best should convey to the child what you want.

## E. Children to Parents

Many passages in the Book of Proverbs begin with the words, "My son." For example, "My son, keep thy father's commandment, and forsake not the law of thy mother: bind them continually upon thine heart, and tie them about thy neck. When thou goest, it shall lead thee; when thou sleepest, it shall keep thee; and when thou awakest, it shall talk with thee" (Proverbs 6:20–22).

Your parents teach you how to relate to life. They teach you why it is wrong to lie or steal. They teach you what evil associations will do to you. They teach about God and about sin. They are very concerned that you learn to relate to God and to others. Your parents are your best friends. Do your part to maintain a good relationship with them.

"Children, obey your parents in the Lord: for this is right. Honour thy father and mother; which is the first commandment with promise; that it may be well with thee, and thou mayest live long on the earth" (Ephesians 6:1–3). This is the child's part in maintaining a good relationship with his parents. This is written to children who are old enough to understand their accountability both to God and to their parents.

*1. From Little Child to Adolescent*

Little children love parents who through nurture and care give them the security they need. They often regard their parents as the best. As they enter their teens, they may reconsider. Their own will and desires become quite important. They pick up ideas from their peers. Their friends outside the family may become their mentors. This may cause trouble in

## Relationships That Bless

the home. It is normal for children to develop relationships outside the home. Although these relationships become important to them, they dare not become more important than their relationship to their parents.

Parents feel differently about this issue. Some are quite concerned that their children fit in with their peers. They go to great lengths to make their children socially acceptable. Other parents are very much the opposite. They are concerned more for the loyalty of their children to themselves as parents. They do not really care whether their children's peers accept them or not. Both of these parental views are extreme.

Children should see their parents as the guiding influence in their lives. Christian parents should be concerned about their children being socially accepted. But they should be more concerned that their children be acceptable to God. In large church communities, it is quite common to have families that are careful with their standards of behavior and other families who are not. Knowing who to be close friends with requires discernment on the part of parents and youth.

Children and youth who want to obey God will face rejection at times by those who are careless. If they have a good relationship with parents who are concerned for their spiritual welfare, it will greatly help. If children regard social acceptance as more important than obedience to parents, it will cause conflicts between them and their parents.

Sometimes children cannot understand why their parents object to something. Even though the parents have tried to explain, it does not seem reasonable. At such times, children are strongly tempted to rebel. They should know that rebellion cuts off a communicating relationship. The rebellious are in trouble not only with parents but also with God.

*2. Responsibility to God Through Parents*

Adolescence is a time when children are becoming responsible not only to parents but also to God. Parents emphasize less what they expect and emphasize more what God expects. They reinforce what they teach with what the Bible says. Ere long the youths will understand that they need the help of God. They will become increasingly aware that their natural desires lead them away from God. Hopefully

## Relationships Within the Family

this will lead them to repentance.

As children become accountable to God, they still have a responsibility to their parents. They must obey them. The Bible commands this. If parents are not Christians, the children must still obey their parents as much as is possible—that is, as long as it does not conflict with what God requires of them.

Parents have years of experience. They know what will be valuable to their children and what will harm them. They have the best interests of their children on their heart. Since this is true, a good relationship with parents has great rewards.

### 3. The Value of Trust

An obedient child is rewarded with trust. A young daughter was once torn between obeying her father and obeying her friend. She had received a letter from her close friend that was not to be shared with anyone. Her father asked to see the letter. The daughter did not want to betray her friend. She brought the letter to her father in little pieces.

The father sought wisdom from God. After consideration, he said to his daughter, "Up to this time, we have trusted you. That trust has been betrayed. No longer will we trust you. We will need to watch you as one who cannot be trusted. However, if you can reproduce that letter in a form that satisfies us that you are revealing its content, we will restore your trust."

No doubt it created a great conflict in the heart of the daughter. Whose trust is more valuable? With whom will she need more to relate? Which relationship is more valuable? Is a person really a friend who would try to get between you and your parents? The daughter decided that the trust of her parents was of greater value than that of her friend. Children must understand this. They value friends. They need friends. But those friends never become more valuable to them than their parents.

### 4. The Secure Child

How does a child know that his parents love him? He knows it by the way he is cared for, but what does that mean? Is a child loved if he is allowed to have his own way? Not really, because in life we must relate to many others. Everyone has ideas, feelings, and desires. These all must at times be given up for the good of another. If a child grows up always having his own way, he will have great difficulty relating to others. A child knows that he is loved when he is not always allowed to have his own way.

Discipline gives the child security. It tells the child that his parents really do care. No matter how much discipline is required to bring a child into subjection, it must be administered. A child cannot have a good relationship with his parents until he willingly submits. Discipline must be severe enough to accomplish cheerful submission.

Each child is different, however, and a parent must discern what type of discipline will bring the best results. Sometimes problems cannot be overcome on one occasion. The rod alone is not necessarily the cure for every problem. Nurture and admonition day after day must accompany discipline. In fact, if we do not give the proper nurture otherwise, the rod can be counterproductive. Sometimes using the rod is the easy way out for parents. Be sure that you are not using the rod to produce in the child what nurture would produce better. Some children do require more severe correction than others; Christian parents need to seek God's direction in bringing the child into subjection.

## F. Grandparents to Children and Grandchildren

Grandparents play a significant role in the life of the family. This is according to God's plan. "Only take heed to thyself, and keep thy soul diligently, lest thou forget the things which thine eyes have seen, and lest they depart from thy heart all the days of thy life: but teach them thy sons, and thy sons' sons" (Deuteronomy 4:9). Grandfathers have a teaching ministry. They are to recount to their children and grandchildren what God did for them. They are to pass on the legacy that they received. They should not let a child or grandchild think that he is fine if he has rejected the teachings of the Bible. They should express their disapproval if their posterity is drifting away from what it was taught.

"Let the elders that rule well be counted worthy of double honour, especially they who labour in the word and doctrine" (1 Timothy 5:17). This verse applies to all older people. The word *especially* singles out the ministers, but it applies to all elders that rule well.\* This does not mean that their rule is arbitrary. What grandparents think about matters should carry some weight. One who rules well is one who commands his children and his household after him. It is indeed a double honor to have children and grandchildren come to grandparents for counsel on any matter of concern. The older ones of the church community should be active in helping to guide the church in spiritual matters. This begins with their place in the family.

"What is an earthquake?" a boy asked his mother. She replied, "Why don't you ask Grandpa about that?" The boy did, and his Grandpa took time to explain that *quake* means "shake," and even shook him just a little to get his point across. This made a lasting and pleasant memory for the grandson.

We live in a time when far too many professing Christians are doing that which is right in their own eyes. Affluence has fertilized the seedbed of apostasy. Many grandparents are indulging in selfish, opulent living. They do as they please and seemingly do not care what their children and grandchildren are doing. Where is the restraining element if grandparents are not seriously and actively involved in the affairs of their children and grandchildren?

## 1. Regaining Lost Respect

Something seems to be seriously missing in the family relationships of America. It shows up in churches as well. *We do not have respect for old age.* We could try to place the blame for this on something or someone, but that is useless. Respect is one of the values that slipped away as affluence made society more independent.

Before we can regain this lost value, we must recognize its absence. Then we must take the steps necessary to regain it over a period of time.

---

\* "Double honour" also refers to remuneration that the church leaders receive.

We did not lose it overnight, and we will not recover it in a day. With repentance on the part of all, God will aid us in regaining it. Where we have failed, we need to lead the way back by giving proper respect to those before us.

"The elders which are among you I exhort, who am also an elder, and a witness of the sufferings of Christ, and also a partaker of the glory that shall be revealed: feed the flock of God which is among you, taking the oversight thereof, not by constraint, but willingly; not for filthy lucre, but of a ready mind; neither as being lords over God's heritage, but being ensamples to the flock" (1 Peter 5:1–3). This we rightfully apply to ministers, but it also applies to all older people. We look to them for an example. They all share in the oversight of the church—if not directly, then indirectly.

"Neither as being lords" has its application. Sometimes older men get the idea that since they are old, their word must carry. This strains relationships. While Peter directed the younger to submit to the elder, he also said "Yea, all of you be subject one to another, and be clothed with humility" (1 Peter 5:5).

*2. Grandpa, Be Humble*

Peter said, "Be clothed with humility" (1 Peter 5:5). We expect grandpas to be humble. Surely, after years under God's corrective hand, they should be. Would to God this were always true. The fact is, they battle the same pride a youngster battles. No one is free from temptation until he dies. Grandpas must guard against the mentality that says "I've been through it all—I know."

If this attitude is associated with a bit of senility, others can smile, forgive, and pray that God would be kind to them. But if we have full use of our minds and yet indulge in proud thoughts about our abilities, we will be difficult to relate to. We should learn to be the kind of grandpa that people want to come to for counsel. We learn this best by being a praying grandpa. If we maintain continual prayer for those under our influence, God will give us a right attitude toward them and toward ourselves.

Relationships Within the Family

## 3. Grandma's Contribution

Grandmas have a distinctive role to fill. "The aged women likewise, that they be in behaviour as becometh holiness, not false accusers, not given to much wine, teachers of good things; that they may teach the young women to be sober, to love their husbands, to love their children, to be discreet, chaste, keepers at home, good, obedient to their own husbands, that the word of God be not blasphemed" (Titus 2:3–5).

This is a great responsibility for grandmas. A lady converted to Christianity lamented that she had had no one to teach her these things. She claimed she had to learn on her own how to love her husband and her children and how to be a discreet, chaste keeper at home. She had no Christian mother or grandmother of her own. Apparently, even when she united with a church, the grandmothers there did not teach her. Some Christian grandmas are not as diligent in their teaching on these matters as they could and should be.

Have we imbibed the idea that times have changed—that we cannot expect granddaughters to have the same values that Grandma had? Does *discreet* mean the same thing to granddaughters that it does to grandmas? Does it have the same practical expression? Does Grandma care or should she care if hemlines rise and fall according to the fads? Should Grandma keep a keen eye on what is modest or immodest and then encourage or rebuke as needed? Yes, Grandma should be involved. She should relate to younger women in a way that helps to keep the church pure and holy.

## 4. Remaining Properly Involved

Older people tend to scale back their involvement in important functions. They are often happy to see younger ones taking up the work. This is as it should be, but those who are older should be involved in giving guidance to those who are doing the work. As the Scriptures indicate, the older ones are to be teachers—teaching the younger ones how to relate to life. They not only teach by words but also by example.

Ezekiel 8 records a sad condition that existed among the old people in Ezekiel's day. Seventy men of the ancients were committing abominations in the dark. Later, God showed Ezekiel twenty-five men who had their backs to the temple and were worshiping the sun. Such grandparents would be hard to respect. "The hoary head is a crown of glory, *if* it be found in the way of righteousness" (Proverbs 16:31).

The Christian family is a tremendous witness for God when parents, children, grandparents, and grandchildren all relate in a harmonious way. God's grace is available to all, and all must use that grace. It is indeed marvelous how God blesses the married couples who fear Him and live for Him. With God's help, they can weather many storms. Each adversity binds the cord tighter, both with God and with each other.

*Chapter Three*

# *Relationships Within the Church*

Good brotherhood relationships are like the chords of a song—they need the careful contribution of all. Since not everyone is careful, discords develop and problems arise. If people ignore problems, they become very serious and can culminate in church divisions. What can we do to avoid carnal strifes among brethren?

Obedience to just a few Biblical principles can make a difference, especially when they are applied early. In the heat of conflict, it is difficult to get people to consider God's will in the matter. For that reason we do well to consider ahead of time what the right course of action will be when we confront a crisis. In this chapter we want to consider the Biblical way to relate to each other in a Christian fellowship.

## A. Leaders to Fellow Leaders

"Likewise, ye younger, submit yourselves unto the elder. Yea, all of you be subject one to another, and be clothed with humility: for God resisteth the proud, and giveth grace to the humble. Humble yourselves therefore under the mighty hand of God, that he may exalt you in due time" (1 Peter 5:5, 6).

## 1. Submission and Humility

We generally think that Christian ministers would be the least likely to have difficulty maintaining good relationships. Probably the opposite is true. They are the most likely to have difficulty.

Several factors contribute to this problem. Ministers are earnest in their study of the Word. They take seriously what they regard as truth. They have vivid memories of lessons learned from experience. What is more, ministers have some authority. They are called of God, and they know it. As a result, they can perceive people who disagree with them as threats to sound doctrine and godly living. What does the Bible say to help leaders find their way through difficulties?

*"Likewise, ye younger, submit yourselves unto the elder."* Reading this, we naturally think of submitting to others ten or twenty years older than ourselves. Let us not forget submission to Christ, "whose goings forth have been from of old, from everlasting" (Micah 5:2). No wonder the New Testament pictures Christ as the head of the church body (1 Corinthians 12; Ephesians 4:11–16) and the chief cornerstone of the church building (Ephesians 2:19–22). Jesus Christ is the elder to whom we all conform and submit. He is the hub of the wheel, the vortex of the whirlpool, the pole toward which all compass needles turn. He is the unity of the church, and the more completely we submit to Him, the more unified we all will be.

In connection with this, we submit to elder brothers in the church. When Paul was converted, he asked the Lord for direction. Jesus could have given directions directly to Paul, but He did not. Rather He said, "Arise, and go into the city, and it shall be told thee what thou must do" (Acts 9:6). This is quite significant. Jesus saw that Paul had been a self-sufficient man, so the first lesson He taught him was to listen to another human, Ananias.

We do not know the age of Ananias, but he was elder to Paul in Christian experience. Ordained men need to defer to other men who have led the church longer than they, especially those who have shown over the years that they have a stable hand on the wheel and a steady eye on the Lord.

*"Yea, all of you be subject one to another."* If anyone had the right not to do this, it would have been the writer himself, Peter. He was one of Christ's "inner circle" and took the foreground at Pentecost and in the early years of the Christian church. Yet when Paul "withstood him to the face" (Galatians 2:11), Peter did not call him junior or upstart, or question his credentials as an apostle. Apparently he took Paul's rebuke like a man. In later years, he even wrote of "our beloved brother Paul" and his wisdom (2 Peter 3:15).

Paul himself was a team player, a fact made more remarkable by the special revelations the Lord gave him. Although in connection with those revelations, he said, "I conferred not with flesh and blood" (Galatians 1:16), for other purposes he did work along with people. When he traveled, he was hardly ever alone. When leaders held a conference in Jerusalem (Acts 15), Paul was there. He mentioned deferring to another church leader with these words: "As touching our brother Apollos, I greatly desired him to come unto you with the brethren: but his will was not at all to come at this time; but he will come when he shall have convenient time" (1 Corinthians 16:12).

This stands in contrast to the elder church leader who saw the decision going against him and finally said, "Well, I guess the elder must submit to the younger!" One of the younger leaders felt stung by this. He had been sent there to help work out a decision with all due respect to the aged but without failing to make his own contribution. The older brother should perhaps have appreciated that contribution more.

*"Be clothed with humility: for God resisteth the proud, and giveth grace to the humble."* At the root of many interpersonal problems lies the sin of pride. In fact, "only by pride cometh contention" (Proverbs 13:10). Leaders are not immune to this. Many of them would admit they must die to their pride every day.

Some leaders have learned from experience that "God resisteth the proud." In dealing with church members, they have faced many frustrations. Personal humiliations have come their way. Leaders who sense that God is resisting them should consider the possibility of pride in their own hearts.

*Relationships That Bless*

We can hardly leave the subject of pride without mentioning jealousy. "Jealousy is cruel as the grave" (Song of Solomon 8:6). Even as the grave cuts off communication, so does jealousy.

Church leaders can easily fall prey to jealousy because they have degrees of power, partly due to position and partly due to personality, and degrees of power can be compared. The twelve disciples, who sensed that power was coming their way, began to argue about who would have the most of it. When James and John tried to capture the largest share in a quick move, the other disciples became indignant (Matthew 20:20–28). Their jealousy over power was no different from that of men in the Roman government. Jesus explained that His kingdom would not operate the way Gentile kingdoms did. His leaders were not to be served, but to serve.

Today we must learn the same lesson. We might be tempted to measure ourselves by the number of wedding sermons we are asked to preach or by the number of times we are called to serve as evangelist out of state or by the number of times we can come up with an idea that others accept in minister's meeting. If we remember that the Lord measures us by a different yardstick, we can relax in our relationships with other leaders and work along with them comfortably.

*2. Sphere of Labor*

Church leaders have different titles that designate their sphere of labor. Bishops have the general oversight of the church. Ministers share in leadership, preaching, and counseling the brotherhood. Deacons oversee the material matters of the church, looking after the needs of the poor and the sick. (Some churches also have leaders called elders.) Although leaders have different offices, they work together, leading the church.

In any group of leaders, one must be the understood senior leader—the one with final authority. In our churches it is the bishop. Without agreement on this arrangement, the leaders will suffer confusion and conflicts. This does not mean the bishop makes all the decisions. Leaders unitedly confront issues and try to discern the will of God together.

If they cannot reach an agreement, they should drop the matter until they can. If time runs out before they reach a decision, the bishop must make it and carry the responsibility for the results.

*3. Analysis of Conflict*

Sometimes there seem to be as many opinions in the room as preachers. There is nothing wrong with this. In fact, thinking together, agreeing and disagreeing, proposing ideas and discarding ideas, and finally coming to an agreement is a very healthy activity. It can have a bonding effect on the group.

But what if leaders set themselves against other leaders and no longer listen to reason? They are losing sight of what is really at stake—the good of the church as a whole. They are failing to remember Christ's earnest prayer "that they all may be one" (John 17:21). Sometimes a situation like this can be redeemed before it descends into permanent bitterness, but sometimes it can split a congregation in two.

When a conflict takes place, is there always wrong on both sides? Quite often there is, but certainly not always. Consider the example of the conflict between Saul and David. Or the one between Moses and Korah. Think of Cain, who became an enemy to Abel. Why? Because Cain's works were evil and his brother's were righteous (1 John 3:12). There can be a clear-cut struggle between truth and error, between righteousness and unrighteousness.

On the other hand, even a minister who is right defeats his own purpose if he piles up evidence to prove that he and he alone is right. He makes matters worse if he also advertises his evidence until he has a sizable following that makes him feel more secure in his thinking. The man who does the most talking brings himself under suspicion, especially if he carries stories that reflect on another's character. Maybe he should begin to suspect that he is not so right as he thought. As someone remarked about an erring brother, "If he's so right, why is he so bent out of shape?"

In a worst-case scenario, the polarization does not confine itself to a single brotherhood, but many people near and far formulate opinions

*Relationships That Bless*

and tell stories that add to the confusion. "Behold, how great a matter a little fire kindleth!" (James 3:5).

How different it might have been if someone had fasted and talked to God instead of to men! God alone has all the facts, and He alone can effectively reason in every individual's heart. In response to prayer, He might not only speak to other people but also to the prayer warrior himself, showing him how best to follow things that make for peace.

It also helps if people give an issue a little rest and do not constantly confront each other about it. Confrontation may have its place, but sometimes a person gets just as far by leaving a brother alone to change his mind when no one is looking. Most of us can recall times when someone kindly contradicted a foolish idea of ours and then changed the subject.

A conflict will continue as long as we focus on the failure of the other as the cause. Saul continued to imagine that David was his enemy even after David had proved that he was his friend. Korah assumed Moses had taken too much upon himself, and nothing Moses said or did could make any difference. "We have met the enemy, and he is us" might apply here.

The humble man accepts the fact that he may be wrong at times. A minister was forcefully confronted after preaching a message on end-time prophecy. The man who confronted him was sure that the minister was wrong. The minister humbly admitted that he could be wrong, but that this was the way he understood it. After the minister admitted that he could be wrong, the other man dropped his head and said, "I guess I could be wrong too."

*4. Maintaining the Union*

In John 17, we read of Jesus praying for the unity of His followers. Where doctrinal purity is not at stake, where there is an obvious desire to be faithful to God, and where there is agreement on applications, the union should be maintained. We all agree that this is true, but what are the keys to this union?

One is love. Everyone makes mistakes that can be interpreted as awful sins by those who hate him. Reading the worst into every situation quickly causes rifts among brethren. But those who love each other forgive mistakes freely, and by doing so, keep unity in the brotherhood.

Love cures fear and suspicion. "There is no fear in love; but perfect love casteth out fear: because fear hath torment. He that feareth is not made perfect in love" (1 John 4:18). We like to think that when we are afraid of someone, it is his fault. If he were different, we would not be afraid of him. Actually, our own lack of love could be the problem.

When we are afraid, we need to consider the words of Isaiah. "I, even I, am he that comforteth you: who art thou, that thou shouldest be afraid of a man that shall die, and of the son of man which shall be made as grass?" (Isaiah 51:12). If we remember that he is a dying man and that we are too, love might come more easily. Remember too, if he is a brother in the church, that we are all working together to forward the kingdom of Jesus. We have nothing to protect but truth and no one to exalt but Jesus.

Another key to unity is the willingness to leave certain matters in God's hands. Matters that pertain to us personally, we can change. But we cannot solve every problem that we might see or think we see in the church. Those issues or people that we cannot change, we leave to God. He can do anything. When we pray in faith, God can change others, or He may change us so we can continue to work together in harmony.

A third key is seeing the value of others' contribution to the cause of Christ. While seeing the value, we should ignore the relative value of each person's contribution. The expression "from the janitor on down to the bishop" reflects this concept. In the end, who cares who is up and who is down? We should avoid comparing the quality of people's work. Who knows with what love it was offered and how warmly it was looked upon in heaven?

A fourth key is willingness to do the part God wants us to do. Good ministerial relationships do not automatically maintain themselves. Each person must conduct himself as a Christian. This involves forgiveness when another fails. It also may involve confronting another minister when he seems to have done wrong, to understand his motives.

Doing what God wants us to do is different from authorizing ourselves to do what we feel like doing. Some people take upon themselves the authority to attack others, and that is quite different from a loving confrontation. When leaders carefully and prayerfully maintain the principles we have examined here, relationships will be valuable and meaningful.

"Blessed are the peacemakers: for they shall be called the children of God" (Matthew 5:9).

## B. Leaders to Followers

*1. The Common Touch*

"Neither as being lords over God's heritage, but being ensamples to the flock" (1 Peter 5:3). The difference between a lord and an example is significant. A lord stands over others, directing them to do things that suit his own pleasure. An example works beside or before others as a pattern to follow.

A spiritual leader must remain on the level with his people. He must understand their struggles. David provided an example of this. Even when he was not yet the established leader, "all Israel and Judah loved David, because he went out and came in before them" (1 Samuel 18:16). Another example was Paul, who said, "Who is weak, and I am not weak? who is offended, and I burn not?" (2 Corinthians 11:29). Paul involved himself in the feelings and experiences of others. He did not meddle in their affairs, but he showed genuine, caring interest.

We relate to others best when we consider them better than ourselves (Philippians 2:3). Most of us are handicapped along this line, however, because we tend to consider ourselves superior to most other people. Surveys have substantiated this. When people were asked to rate themselves in comparison to others, by far the majority rated themselves above average. I do not know if any of those surveyed were Christians. But it does show what we think naturally.

Someone summarized this attitude neatly with the tongue-in-cheek statement "It is hard to soar with eagles when you have to work with turkeys." The trap here is that as long as we have this kind of attitude, people will not be comfortable with us. They might even call our attitude by its right name—pride.

It may be of great value to ask another brother if he sees evidences of pride in our life. For the right kind of help, we must make sure it is an unbiased brother who will be honest with us. Then we should accept his evaluation and humbly admit our exposed pride, repent of it, and forsake it. If he obviously has misunderstood us and falsely accused us, we must simply dismiss it and forgive. Keeping quiet and allowing God to vindicate us (if need be) goes far in helping to maintain good relationships with those under our direction.

*2. Acceptance*

Leaders must relate to many kinds of personalities. Some of them refresh us whenever we meet them; others drain us. It is possible for us to wish that certain people were not under our care. If we become aware that this feeling has crept into our hearts, we must repent and thank God for each brother and sister He has given us. People quickly sense acceptance or rejection, even if we never say a word about it to them, and it makes a difference in how they relate to us.

Rejection is right for those who are disobedient (2 Thessalonians 3:14). This should only take place after they are excommunicated from the brotherhood. Even then the type of rejection can be wrong. Contemptuous rejection comes from a proud heart. It causes one to despise and ridicule another. It builds walls instead of bridges. It is carnal in every outworking. We must repent and make restitution if we have had such attitudes. May God spare leaders from rejecting souls for such selfish reasons.

After Paul told the Thessalonians not to keep company with the disobedient, he told them not to count them as enemies but to warn them as brethren. That is the right kind of rejection—the kind that offers complete acceptance as soon as it becomes possible.

*3. Confidentiality*

Individuals feel differently about their personal matters. Some easily share with others what they are experiencing. Others feel that their personal life is no one else's business. These varying personality traits affect how people think about money matters, health matters, family matters, and social matters.

Christian leaders need to continually pray for wisdom to know how to help the many kinds of people under their care. On the one hand, they have the privacy of the people to protect. On the other hand, they have the purity of the church to maintain. Leaders need to discern why people want to be secretive about their lives. Do they have a natural desire for privacy, or do they have things to hide?

Financial matters can be delicate to deal with. If a brother is a poor steward or makes a financial blunder, how much should we say? Maybe to avoid singling him out, we can speak in general terms over the pulpit—but we dare not make him feel singled out over the pulpit. Yet to say nothing at all might be wrong too, for we have an obligation to him—if not as an ordained man, at least as a brother. In many cases, friendly, private conversation illuminated with stories from our own experience is a good approach.

Ministers fare best when they commit the whole issue to God from the beginning. In His own way, God will make clear what is the right way to relate to these people. Sometimes they need active intervention, but other times they do not.

We leaders need to teach and exemplify the value of being open one with another. Being open does not mean that we share every detail of our lives, but it does mean that we let people know we have struggles like they do.

With some effort and planning, leaders can maintain a valued exchange with those under their care. Some followers will express their thinking and feelings without much prodding. Others will not share their thoughts unless they know that we really want to know what they think. Yet each member needs to feel appreciated—that what he thinks is important.

*4. Trust*

When we trust people, we convey that trust by the way we treat them. Trusting them can be hard, however, if they betray our trust. When this happens, we can do one of two things. We can forgive on the basis that they meant well and the error was unintentional. This puts us back on the road to trust again. Or we can confront them as directed by Galatians 6:1: "Restore such an one in the spirit of meekness." Here too we can regain our trust in them and treat them confidently once more.

There is, of course, a third option. We can say, "That's a real disappointment; now I know I cannot trust him any more." From that point on, we can add incident to incident to prove the untrustworthiness of that person. Certainly we know that some people are on their way out of the church and that no amount of goodwill on our part will stop them. But we are speaking here of someone who does seem to want to do right. Let us not break the bruised reed or quench the smoking flax (Matthew 12:20).

It takes a long time for some people to grow up. But it took a long time for us to grow up too, and the people who treated us with friendly warmth all the while, giving us the benefit of the doubt, did much for us.

We build confidence by including our brethren when we make decisions. When leaders take weighty matters to the brotherhood and allow them to help chart a course of action, it builds mutual trust. If members sense that leaders do not trust them, how will they trust leaders?

One small congregation had only one ordained leader for several years. During that time the leader counseled often with the brethren. As the congregation grew, another leader was added. Together the leaders decided some issues, but they continued to seek advice from the brotherhood. As the congregation prepared for the third ordination, a brother sounded this warning: "When you get too many men in the leadership, they become cliquish. They make decisions among themselves and do not maintain the valued exchange with the brotherhood that was experienced when there was only one ordained man." That brother had a valuable point.

Even though we have what we consider a full ministry, let us not forget the value of including the brotherhood in making decisions. Give them the opportunity to express their views. Give the brotherhood the opportunity to hear what the others think. Leaders should have some idea what conclusions should be made. They should have Scriptures to substantiate their desired conclusion. However, they should be open to change if a spiritual discussion leads otherwise.

I remember one such incident in our brotherhood. We live in a community where there are different kinds of Mennonite churches. In any given locality, you may have as many as four different Mennonite neighbors. One of these neighbors decided to have a chicken barbecue and invited all the other Mennonite neighbors. This involved several from our congregation. One of our families did not think we should participate in a mixed social activity like this. The others did not see anything too serious about it. Since there were different opinions among those invited, they consulted the ministers. After some deliberation, the ministers decided that probably attending would do no harm. But since it did involve several families, and since they did not agree, they thought it might be well to discuss it with the brotherhood. This they did.

When the matter was presented, several other brethren objected. They noted that the different groups had different ideals for their children and their youth. Associations solely on a social level would be more harmful than helpful. Their reasons were both logical and Biblical. After the discussion, the brotherhood chose a safe course and everyone was satisfied.

Several elements must be present for such a meeting to benefit the brotherhood. Every brother must be spiritually-minded. None dare have an agenda to promote. Each must want the will of the Lord. In the aforementioned meeting, there was no question about the spiritual desire of every brother.

What a blessing to see leaders and other brethren drawing together in confidence as they together make decisions in the fear of God.

## C. Followers to Leaders

Relationship problems frequently develop between sheep and shepherds. The Bible provides many examples of this type of problem. We want to explore the Christian way for followers to relate to leaders.

"Remember them which have the rule over you, who have spoken unto you the word of God: whose faith follow, considering the end of their conversation" (Hebrews 13:7). "Obey them that have the rule over you, and submit yourselves: for they watch for your souls, as they that must give account, that they may do it with joy, and not with grief: for that is unprofitable for you" (Hebrews 13:17). "And we beseech you, brethren, to know them which labour among you, and are over you in the Lord, and admonish you; and to esteem them very highly in love for their work's sake. And be at peace among yourselves" (1 Thessalonians 5:12, 13).

These verses provide the recipe for good relationships with leaders. If we practice these three things—remember, obey, and esteem—we will have a blessed relationship with leaders.

*1. Remember, Obey, Esteem*

In what way do we *remember* our leaders? We remember leaders by praying for them continually. We remember them as we follow their faith and example. We remember them by seeing that their physical needs are met. We remember them by being supportive. This calls for self-sacrifice but affords a great deal of satisfaction.

To what extent are we required to *obey* leaders? Does God expect us to blindly obey them? Jesus said, "The scribes and the Pharisees sit in Moses' seat: all therefore whatsoever they bid you observe, that observe and do; but do not ye after their works: for they say, and do not" (Matthew 23:2, 3).

Jesus was speaking to people under the Jewish Law. His kingdom today operates from a completely different standpoint. Yet some principles remain the same. His kingdom is composed of people having leaders. We can submit even to bad leaders and be right with God. We can also submit to good leaders and be wrong. (The Jewish leaders did things to be seen of men. That was wrong. We can submit to leaders to be seen of men. This is also wrong.) Christians, because they fear God, submit to their leaders.

Where leaders watch for your soul, their leadership will benefit you only if you cheerfully submit to them. Cheerful submission creates a beautiful working relationship. If we add positive support to cheerful obedience, we create a bond very difficult for the devil to penetrate.

True Christians *esteem* their leaders very highly in love for their work's sake. Why does God ask us to do this to men? After all, they are only men just like everyone else. The Bible provides the answer: "for their work's sake." It is not necessarily the quantity of work they do, but whose work it is. Leading the church is God's work.

Is this esteem for the leader's benefit? No, this high esteem benefits the one who esteems. Not only will the leader enjoy a good relationship with us, but we will also enjoy a good relationship with him.

Will leaders get proud if all their followers esteem them highly? Actually, high esteem humbles true Christian leaders. They sense that it is not their own good work; God is working in the hearts of their followers. When we remember, obey, and esteem leaders, we benefit, those around us benefit, and those who are over us benefit. Most of all, God is glorified when we maintain a Scriptural relationship with our leaders.

*2. The Human Dimension*

Leaders are men, and they make mistakes. This can be very difficult to relate to. We want a leader who can always be trusted. If a man makes one mistake, he probably will make another one. How can we trust a man who makes mistakes? The problem becomes especially difficult if the man does not recognize his errors.

We must remember several things. How do we decide if a leader has done wrong? Many times it is a matter of interpretation. Judging motives is especially dangerous and usually involves judging in a carnal way that Jesus forbids. "Judge not, that ye be not judged. For with what judgment ye judge, ye shall be judged: and with what measure ye mete, it shall be measured to you again. And why beholdest thou the mote that is in thy brother's eye, but considerest not the beam that is in thine own eye?" (Matthew 7:1–3). Paul addresses the same problem in Romans 2:1–11. It is very natural for us to judge because we are sinners by nature. For the same reason, it is very natural for our judgments to be wrong.

Jesus did teach us to beware of false prophets (Matthew 7:15–20). Men do not gather grapes of thorns or figs of thistles. If selfishness and pride dominate a man's character, he is a false prophet. However, it is not right to judge a leader to be false because of an isolated failure. In fact, if in general a leader is faithful, our judgment of an isolated incident may well be wrong.

Real problems develop when our own pride and selfishness force us into a conflict with our leader. If pride and hatred darken our heart, we can construe almost any act to be evil. Men did it to Jesus. They did it to many faithful men in history. We ought to be afraid to put ourselves in conflict with leaders.

Murmuring against leaders is an old sin. It makes us feel good when we can point out the flaws and failures of those over us. The story of Korah's conduct recorded in Numbers 16 might seem far from our situation, but any rebellion against leadership carries the same elements. First the leaders are accused of taking too much upon themselves. "All Christians have the Holy Spirit," we hear. "All Christians have direct contact with God. Leaders should not make decisions without consulting the brotherhood." The next accusation is that leaders lift themselves above the congregation. When you make this kind of accusation or hear it from others, beware!

Were Korah and his company in opposition to Moses? They thought they were. But they were actually in opposition to themselves. They were doing themselves irreparable damage. Paul told Timothy to meekly instruct "those that oppose themselves; if God peradventure will give them repentance to the acknowledging of the truth" (2 Timothy 2:25). When we put ourselves in conflict with those who are over us in the Lord, we are against ourselves. We are not acting in our own best interest.

The Christian who enjoys sweet communion with God is not easily perturbed by the mistakes of his leaders. He is quick to talk to God about it because he knows that God can do anything. One Christian couple was troubled by a decision their leaders had made. They were quite sure that it was not for the good of the congregation. They also sensed that they would not be understood if they raised objection. They decided to take the matter to the Lord and leave it with Him. It was only a matter of weeks until circumstances made it impossible for the leaders' decision to be implemented. They simply got on their knees and thanked God for His faithfulness.

God can do marvelous things if we get out of the way and stay out of the way. God is not glorified when we think we must help Him keep leaders straight. Let me illustrate. God called a deacon to work with a bishop who was quite different from him in his view of money matters. The bishop was tight and the deacon was loose. For some reason, the deacon began thinking that God had put him with this bishop to balance the bishop. Consequently, instead of being supportive, the deacon often worked against the bishop on money issues. After all, the deacon's calling was in money matters.

You can imagine the conflict that grew until the bishop decided it had gone too far. With the permission of the deacon, he asked several brethren to come together to hear the problem. After hearing the case, the brethren commended them for having kept the problem between themselves. Then they gave recommendations for both sides.

During the meeting, God showed the deacon that he had not been called to serve with his bishop for the purpose of changing him. He began to realize that God had called this bishop to his work, and God would deal with the bishop without his help. They forgave each other and began to work together. Today, from all evidence, they enjoy a blessed relationship of love and respect.

How different it would have been if they had not repented and forgiven each other! This situation took place between ordained leaders, but it can happen among others if any brother gets the idea that he is God's man to straighten out a leader.

It is wrong for us to think that God is depending on us to help another man overcome his flaws, rather than seeing ourselves as part of a reciprocal brotherhood. That kind of thinking destroys relationships. First of all we are not thinking rightly about ourselves. Also we are not thinking rightly about our brother, and we are not thinking rightly about God.

When we focus on the faults of our leaders, we are not considering our own weaknesses. When the Jews brought an adulterous woman to Jesus, asking what should be done to her, Jesus turned the spotlight on their own hearts. "He that is without sin among you, let him first cast a stone at her" (John 8:7). Paul directed the Galatians to meekly consider themselves when they were about to help another overcome his faults (Galatians 6:1). When we honestly consider ourselves, we must conclude that we are no better than anyone else. We all need the mercy of Jesus.

It is wrong to rebuke elders, but we may entreat them as fathers (1 Timothy 5:1). The difference between rebuke and entreaty is drastic. One comes from a heart of love, and the other comes from some other emotion. If people would only stop and consider what they do to themselves when they allow feelings other than love to permeate their lives. This is especially true when it involves their relationship with their leaders.

True Christians believe that prayer changes people. It (God actually) changes us first of all, and that is most important. Prayer changes our attitude about ourselves and about others. Let us be humble enough to turn matters over to God and maintain a sweet relationship with Him, and then we will enjoy good relationships with others.

"Great peace have they which love thy law: and nothing shall offend them" (Psalm 119:165).

## D. Brother to Brother

"As we have therefore opportunity, let us do good unto all men, especially unto them who are of the household of faith" (Galatians 6:10).

"Let nothing be done through strife or vainglory; but in lowliness of mind let each esteem other better than themselves" (Philippians 2:3).

"And be ye kind one to another, tenderhearted, forgiving one another, even as God for Christ's sake hath forgiven you" (Ephesians 4:32).

"Put on therefore, as the elect of God, holy and beloved, bowels of mercies, kindness, humbleness of mind, meekness, longsuffering; forbearing one another, and forgiving one another, if any man have a quarrel against any: even as Christ forgave you, so also do ye. And above all these things put on charity, which is the bond of perfectness. And let the peace of God rule in your hearts, to the which also ye are called in one body; and be ye thankful" (Colossians 3:12–15).

Three elements stand out in these verses: humility, love, and forgiveness. Without these three Christian graces, true Christian brotherhood cannot exist. Many church communities do exist without them, but they are maintained by hypocrisy. People pretend to be humble. They feign their love, and they claim to forgive. For that reason, given the right set of circumstances, a crisis can develop that splits the community.

If this would only happen to one in a thousand church communities, we could pass it by as incidental. But it happens over and over again, and we are forced to face some facts. The commonness of divisions in religious circles should not cause us to shrug our shoulders and say, "So what, everybody else is doing it." Should we be satisfied with such juvenility? There is a better way. Paul called it the "more excellent way"— the way of love. Jesus said, "A new commandment I give unto you, That ye love one another; as I have loved you, that ye also love one another. By this shall all men know that ye are my disciples, if ye have love one to another" (John 13:34, 35).

Remember, we can only love as Jesus loved if we have experienced the new birth. Without the Holy Spirit, it is impossible to have the supernatural love of Jesus. Nor can we escape from social evils even if we have been warned about them.

## 1. The Reality of Hypocrisy

Life is full of interaction with people. Christians are in the world as sheep among wolves. We can expect to be hated, mistreated, and despised. Within the true Christian brotherhood, it is quite different. But it will only be different if every brother bears his cross and crucifies the flesh every day in every experience. Even in the church, we all face temptations to pride, hatred, and rejection of others. Being human, we will all be disappointed in others at times. If we forgive our brother and continue to love him, we maintain our peace. If we yield to the temptation to despise him, our peace vanishes, and a whole set of other emotions takes over.

In that emotional upheaval, few Christians are honest. We deny our true feelings. We know God requires us to love. We know that we do not love that brother the way we used to, but we still love him—some. The devil aids us in justifying our feelings. It is all very reasonable. How different it is when we get down on our knees immediately and ask God to take the hatred out of our hearts, and then let Him do it. If we deny our hatred, we lose our relationship with both God and our brother. "If we say that we have no sin, we deceive ourselves, and the truth is not in us. If we confess our sins, he is faithful and just to forgive us our sins, and to cleanse us from all unrighteousness" (1 John 1:8, 9).

If we do not properly deal with our hurts, we soon enter the realm of hypocrisy. We pretend that we love when we do not love. We might even do things to try to prove to ourselves and to others that we still love, but the veneer is easily scratched. There is no substitute for true Christlike forgiveness "if any man have a quarrel against any."

2. *The Forgiveness Imperative*

When Jesus taught us to pray, He included the matter of forgiveness. We are to pray, "Forgive us our debts, as we forgive our debtors" (Matthew 6:12). That phrase was the only part of the prayer that He explained. If we do not forgive others, God will not forgive us.

In Matthew 18:23–35, Jesus told a story that illustrates the incongruity of our unforgiveness. He said someone who had been forgiven a great unpayable debt went out and took a fellow servant by the throat and demanded payment of a small debt. When the fellow servant pled for mercy, the first man would not grant him mercy. In the end the first one incurred his whole debt upon himself again. It seems incredible that someone would do this, but Jesus said, "Likewise shall my heavenly Father do also unto you, if ye from your hearts forgive not every one his brother their trespasses."

One sobering detail stands out at the beginning of Jesus' story. He said that the kingdom of heaven is like this. This kind of thing does happen among Christians. It is serious because we lose our salvation if we do not forgive.

We deceive ourselves by claiming that we forgive, when we do not actually forgive. When we forgive we do not demand satisfaction for an offense. We give up all resentment towards another person. We grant him free pardon. That is what God does for all who repent.

Jesus prayed, "Father, forgive them; for they know not what they do" (Luke 23:34). That prayer indicates that Jesus was completely free of hatred toward His enemies. Those enemies never experienced the peace of forgiveness until they repented, but that was not Jesus' fault. It is the same in human relationships. Friendship cannot be restored until an enemy has repented of his animosity, but in the meantime we can forgive.

Forgiveness is never dependent on the other person. No one can keep us from forgiving another. Neither can another person force us to forgive someone. No one can keep us from loving him. Neither can anyone compel us to love him. God Himself will not. Nevertheless, we are all accountable to God for what we carry in our hearts, whether love or hatred, whether forgiveness or unforgiveness. We cannot blame others for the way we feel.

Sometimes we remember things we thought we had forgiven and put out of our mind. Does that mean we have not forgiven? Not really, but it does mean that again we need to commit the whole issue to the Lord and rest in the fact that He knows all about it. We also ask God to deliver us from any resentment that may arise in our heart.

If in our remembering we again go through all the injustices of the incident, we probably have not forgiven the offender. Likewise, if we find it easy to detail the incident to another person, we have not forgiven. A brief remembrance that causes us to recall God's redemptive deliverance can be of value. It leaves us free to think lovingly and compassionately of the one who wronged us.

God forgives us and puts our sins far away—as far as the east is from the west (Psalm 103:12). "For I will be merciful to their unrighteousness, and their sins and their iniquities will I remember no more" (Hebrews 8:12). But if we do not continue to forgive others, our sins will come against us again. (See Matthew 18:35.)

Forgiveness is not natural. But the Holy Spirit now rules our hearts, and He gives us the power to do that which is beyond natural inclination. We are new creatures in Christ, and we forgive as Christ forgave.

How we feel in our hearts affects how we relate to others. It is not just fellow church members who can sense how we feel toward them. Often non-Christians can too. That is why Jesus said, "By this shall all men know that ye are my disciples, if ye have love one to another" (John 13:35). It cannot be hidden.

*3. Proper Esteem of Others*

Esteeming others better than ourselves requires divine grace. The more we practice this esteem, the more valuable it becomes to us. We cannot begin to do this until we have discovered the wickedness of our own hearts. "The heart is deceitful above all things, and desperately wicked: who can know it?" (Jeremiah 17:9).

True self-discovery humbles us. Since we can know more about our own badness than we can about anyone else's, we can esteem other people better than ourselves. This is a far better reaction to our own weaknesses than exposing the weaknesses of others to boost our own pride.

To esteem others better than ourselves, we must consider their value to us. Friendships are valuable. The more diverse our circle of friends, the greater will be their value to us. With God's help we can even learn to appreciate those little quirks that make some people seem a bit odd. How could we develop patience if others responded to us just the way we want them to? How could we learn forgiveness if no one disappointed us? How could we ever learn compassion if there were no needy families?

We can learn to see valuable characteristics in every brother. Instead of gossiping about the failures of others, we talk about the good contribution others make to us. Where brethren esteem others better than themselves, true brotherhood will thrive. Without it the brotherhood will be no more than a religious fraternity.

The Apostle Paul's prayer for the Philippians gives us the elements of this esteem of others. "And this I pray, that your love may abound yet more and more in knowledge and in all judgment; that ye may approve things that are excellent; that ye may be sincere and without offence till the day of Christ; being filled with the fruits of righteousness, which are by Jesus Christ, unto the glory and praise of God" (Philippians 1:9–11).

Note the elements in this prayer.

First, love abounds in knowledge. Often, the more we know about another person the less we love him. It should not be this way. A marriage is successful when a couple's love grows as their knowledge of each other increases. This knowledge includes all the weaknesses and failures of each other. The discovery that our mates are very human makes us feel free to be human and completely open. On the other hand, couples who expect perfection in their mates are soon disappointed and begin to stack up memories of failure upon failure until there is an explosion. Unless someone reverses the process, it is only a matter of time until a divorce takes place.

The same principle applies to the brotherhood. We are all human, and we all make mistakes. This knowledge should make us free to be ourselves—to be free within the standard of righteousness. Likewise, where love abounds in spite of (or because of) what we know, it will temper how we judge another.

Next, love abounds in judgment. The husband who loves his wife as Christ loved the church will always judge his wife in the most favorable light. As a result, his love for her will continue to grow. The same thing happens in the church. We see people's qualities in a favorable light. In other words, we "approve things that are excellent."

Most people, if not all, have an excelling virtue. For some we may need to watch closely to find it. Having found it, we should approve it and tell others about it. This promotes good relationships. Too naturally we see the things that are not excellent, and we often get quite vocal about the failure of others—especially if they are leaders. Who has ever improved brotherhood relationships by magnifying the faults of others? Why not do as Paul directs? Focus on the things that are excellent and help to build good relationships.

Remember, in order to enjoy good relationships, be sincere. By nature we pretend. We have lost our childhood candor. We have learned what is expected of us, and we feign obedience whether we believe in our heart or not. This insincerity is sin. Unless we repent of it, we will lose our relationship with God and our brethren.

*4. Relating to the Weak*

"Him that is weak in the faith receive ye, but not to doubtful disputations" (Romans 14:1).

"We then that are strong ought to bear the infirmities of the weak, and not to please ourselves" (Romans 15:1).

"Now we exhort you, brethren, warn them that are unruly, comfort the feebleminded, support the weak, be patient toward all men" (1 Thessalonians 5:14).

"To the weak became I as weak, that I might gain the weak: I am made all things to all men, that I might by all means save some" (1 Corinthians 9:22).

Weak. Strong. Is it right to categorize people this way? Is it right to categorize ourselves? Yes, facts are facts, and on various points we are either weak or strong. Accordingly, we find ourselves under obligation to God and to one another. If we want to think of ourselves as strong, we have a duty to the weak. If we see ourselves as weak, we have obligations as well.

Before we discuss the weak, we should make an important distinction between the weak and the carnal.

A weak person has faith, but he suffers from doubts about what is acceptable to God and what is not. He is troubled about many little details and sometimes overemphasizes them in comparison to more important doctrines. For instance, Paul mentioned the observance of days and diet. Some Christians feel strongly about not working on Christmas Day or Good Friday or Ascension Day. Others are just as careful *not* to observe these days, associating them with idolatry. Some Christians feel strongly that we should be careful to eat wholesome, "organic" foods.

In contrast, the carnal person loves himself and loves the world. He is not as concerned about pleasing God as about pleasing himself. His self-love does not stem from weak faith but from sin. If he quibbles about details, it is not from a desire to do right but from a desire to look spiritual. Such a person must be rebuked, and if he does not repent, he must be excluded from the brotherhood.

Coming back to the weak, the relationship problem between them and the strong is found in Romans 14:3: "Let not him that eateth despise him that eateth not; and let not him which eateth not judge him that eateth: for God hath received him." The strong are tempted to despise the weak. The weak are tempted to judge the strong. When either the weak or the strong yield to their temptation, relationship problems develop.

Three more principles come into focus in Romans 14. The first is found in verse 8: "We are the Lord's." We need to consider how the things we do will affect our relationship to God. Will God be pleased if I spend twelve to fifteen thousand dollars on a vehicle to drive to town when a vehicle worth half that much would do it? Not that we must be in constant turmoil over what we should or should not do. Rather, as we grow in grace and in our knowledge of God, we will more and more automatically consult God about all matters.

The second principle has to do with oneself. Verse 12 states it this way: "So then every one of us shall give account of himself to God." When we finally stand before God, will our choices have built us up spiritually? Since the spiritual life is ever changing—maturing or dwindling—every choice must be made in the light of what it will do to us spiritually. Are we growing in grace (2 Peter 3:18), or are we becoming carnal (Romans 8:6)?

The third principle involves our brother. Will the things we do cause him to stumble? If so, those things are wrong for us. This principle can become quite confining to us, or at least seem that way. We might argue that some little thing we do should not be a stumbling block to anyone. Nevertheless, God is watching, and if we "offend one of these little ones" (Matthew 18:6), we will give account to Him.

When it came to food, Paul said in effect, "It is all a matter of how you look at it." In his own words, "I know, and am persuaded by the Lord Jesus, that there is nothing unclean of itself: but to him that esteemeth any thing to be unclean, to him it is unclean" (Romans 14:14).

Does this principle apply to food only? No, Paul also mentioned keeping holidays. But it is hard to think of more examples that will not offend any readers. Things that some Christians would call clean might be esteemed unclean by others.

Some items of personal appearance might belong in this category. Suppose a family moves to a more conservative congregation than the one they came from. They should make adjustments that help them fit in with what people there expect, even though they themselves have no scruples on the matter.

Suppose again that in an informal situation, one brother might habitually open his collar. While spending time with another brother who keeps his closed, he might stay buttoned up too. At least he would if that would improve the comfort level between the two of them. Many a brother would shrug over the small liberties another enjoys and say, "Let every man be fully persuaded in his own mind" (Romans 14:5).

Pastimes might be an illustration. A brother might go hunting because he can usually make the time and investment pay in terms of meat in the freezer. To him it seems to be good stewardship. But if congregational feeling, for sensible reasons or not, is strong against hunting, he should consider selling his gun and explaining to his boys that relationships are more important than pheasants or venison.

Ordained men and their families face more constraints along this line than others do. They must be "all things to all men" even more than most other Christians. An unordained brother might feel free to attend

## Relationships That Bless

a meeting of feed salesmen or beekeepers or fruit producers. A minister might or might not. At the very least he should think twice, remembering to stand back and see himself as others see him.

One caution: no one should assume that since "there is nothing unclean of itself," he may privately indulge in sin. That is not the point at all. Paul was not whitewashing uncleanness, which he lists in Galatians 5:19 along with adultery and fornication and lasciviousness.

It is also wrong to assume from verse 14 that as long as one's conscience does not bother him about some item, it must be all right. "That doesn't trouble me" is not the final judge of right and wrong. The Word of God is.

Consider this too: most of us like to classify ourselves as strong. Let us just remember that the line between "strong" and "carnal" can be pretty fine. If a "strong" Christian scoffs at the scruples of a weak brother, he proves himself more carnal than strong.

Finally, those brethren we consider weak are good for us. Envision a brotherhood of all strong Christians, where no one needed to exercise patience and forbearance. How could the brotherhood mature properly? Jesus designed the body to have feeble parts because feeble parts are necessary (1 Corinthians 12:22).

Besides, a brother we consider weak might be drawing a line that we will eventually see is important. We need to draw it too. He was the strong brother all the time.

### 5. The Biblical Solution

God lays the responsibility of good relationships upon all. Let us consider further Biblical teaching on the matter. Jesus said, "Therefore if thou bring thy gift to the altar, and there rememberest that thy brother hath ought against thee; leave there thy gift before the altar, and go thy way; first be reconciled to thy brother, and then come and offer thy gift" (Matthew 5:23–24).

Later Jesus said, "Moreover if thy brother shall trespass against thee, go and tell him his fault between thee and him alone: if he shall hear thee, thou hast gained thy brother. But if he will not hear thee, then take with thee one or two more, that in the mouth of two or three witnesses every word may be established. And if he shall neglect to hear them, tell it unto the church: but if he neglect to hear the church, let him be unto thee as an heathen man and a publican" (Matthew 18:15–17).

Both of these Scripture passages indicate that relationship problems are to be handled with dispatch. Do not even give an offering if you remember that someone has something against you. This is not a matter that can wait until just before Communion. You take care of it right now. Leave the gift at the altar and first be reconciled, and then come back and offer your gift.

The Greek word translated *reconciled* has the thought of being changed thoroughly. This does not mean that you go and get the person changed in his thinking toward you. It is not a matter of getting him to see that he is wrong in having something against you. Self-defending confessions do not restore relationships. If you know someone has something against you, find out what it is and why. Then acknowledge your humanness. If it was unintentional, say so, but do not deny your fault. Ask what you can do to make amends. A bishop brother says it is helpful if he can find something else on his own side that was not right and acknowledge it. He says that really warms people up.

The Matthew 18 passage teaches how to deal with someone who trespasses against us. First, go tell him about it. Try to convey it in a way that will let him know you want good relationships. Remember that this is a matter between you and him alone. If you cannot get it off your mind, do not tell someone else about it. Tell him. If he refuses to hear you, then take one or two more. If he refuses to hear them, tell it to the church leaders. It must be brought to a conclusion.

When we know that something has come between us and another brother or sister, sometimes we are tempted to think that we do not need a good relationship with that brother or sister. This is not true. We cannot have a good relationship with God until all relationships with men are as good as we can make them.

Either way, whether someone has something against us or has trespassed against us, we are responsible to deal with it. We should not say,

"If he has something against me, he can come to me." Neither should we say, "He knows he offended me; when he repents, he can come and tell me." Keeping peace in the church is every person's business, especially our own.

### E. Sister to Sister

The Biblical principles that govern relationships among brethren apply to sisters also. This is not surprising, for women face many of the same pitfalls.

Women are different from each other just as men are different from each other. God meant this diversity for good, but it carries the potential for friction, resentment, and even bitterness. In order for their diverse personalities to bring out the best in each other, women need to be transformed by God and filled with His supernatural love.

But women are unlike men in other ways—thankfully! As a rule, they seem more spiritually sensitive. Although a few of them seem able to fall further than men into broken relationships, some also seem able to rise higher than men in forgiveness, forbearance, compassion, and longsuffering.

*1. The Matter of Talk*

To a somewhat greater degree than men, women create and solve their problems with talk. In this, therefore, they are both better and worse than men. They can more easily express themselves, but they can more easily express the wrong thing. Since talk is a fair portion of a woman's life, we will address the subject here. (The men need not stop reading.)

The first person to talk to about anything is the Lord. He is "a very present help" *before* we get into trouble by saying the wrong thing. Think about all the good that could be accomplished if we would go to the secret closet and talk to God about people and refuse to talk about people to others. Think what good we would do by lifting our hearts to the Lord when the telephone rings. "Lord, help me say the right thing and know when to quit" might be an appropriate prayer. Most of us have seen firsthand the damage done to churches and individuals by gossip, and we must not be a party to it.

Then too, we have that wonderful opportunity to pray for the forgiveness of another's sin (1 John 5:16). If we really love someone, that is what we will do. We will not whisper behind our hands about what we saw or thought we saw. Instead, we will implore God to forgive them because we know that they really want to do what is right. This is fervent charity, and it covers a multitude of sins (1 Peter 4:8).

2. *Pride and Envy*

Women have to guard against sins of the spirit. Envy and pride can plague them. The efficient woman with everything under control might enjoy comparing her house to the cluttered house of her sister down the road. If she has time to help others with their work, she might feel the urge to mention it at sewing circle. (Many of us have heard of name-droppers; there are accomplishment-droppers too.) Promoting ourselves is a symptom of pride.

On the other hand, the woman who flies around the house but never seems to catch up might mentally grumble about the sister who always seems to be done with everything. "How can she do it? I wonder what corners she cuts. Of course she doesn't have as many children as I do, and I guess she never had a fussy baby, and if she hadn't talked to me so long yesterday, I'd have gotten more done." And on and on. Envy!

All people have limitations. Our own limitations should refute our pride, and other people's limitations should refute our envy. Maybe we should simply stop thinking so much about our limitations. People who resent their own deficiencies simply make us aware of them. How much better it would be if they would rejoice in the Lord and focus on Him rather than on themselves!

3. *Friendships*

Christian women benefit by maintaining a wide circle of friends. Close friends are valuable, but cliques result from selfishness and deprive people of the perspective that having many friends could give them. There is a place for a long, intense conversation with one person. But there are more places (after church, for instance) to keep in touch with many people.

Women naturally have their own interests and like to share them with other women. Mothers with babies love to compare the progress of their children. They can profitably exchange many child-training experiences. Gardening ideas along with other housekeeping hints can be passed around. Of course, no one should make her own way appear to be the only right way. But mothers should be discreet in what, when, and where they share with other women about birthing experiences and intimate relationships. Some things are best kept between them and their husbands.

Sometimes people enter the church fellowship who have not been trained in arts such as homemaking, gardening, and sewing. If women spend too much time talking about these things, these individuals might begin to feel very inadequate. Show interest in how *they* cope with life. Sometimes drop the Martha talk for a while and follow Mary's example. Remember, the bond that holds you and your sisters together is not the practical interests, but the fact that you all sit at the feet of Jesus.

## 4. *The Older Teaching the Younger*

The Bible directs aged women to "teach the young women to be sober, to love their husbands, to love their children, to be discreet, chaste, keepers at home, good, obedient to their own husbands" (Titus 2:3–5). Some things the young women will learn by experience, but some things they should be taught. Why? For instance, why must young women be taught to love their husbands?

Young married couples sometimes become frustrated as they try to understand each other. Since men and women view life from different perspectives, misunderstandings may arise. The once-loving young husband can appear to be very thoughtless. How will the young wife know what to do in such times? Will she begin to despise the young man she once adored? Is that not what he deserves?

In a situation like this, an older successful Christian wife or mother can be very helpful. She should be able to explain that a man thinks differently from a woman. She can tell the young sister how to draw from her husband the love and affection she desires. An older woman can help a younger one understand that a loving wife is much happier than a resentful one. A wife can function more freely without the added weight of self-pity.

Lamentably, not all senior women have made a success of their marital. Not all can give helpful advice. If you need counsel, seek someone who has had a good marital relationship.

5. *The Snares in Books*

Today we can purchase many books on child training and marital relationships. Depending solely on books bypasses the healthy exchange that God planned between older and younger women. Also, many of these books are not Biblically sound.

Sometimes unsolicited information comes in the mail on such matters. When this happens, a young sister should seek out an older sister and get her opinion on things that sound questionable. This does not mean she should avoid discussing such matters with her husband. In fact she *should* talk to him. But if she wants a sister's opinion in addition to that of her husband, it should be from someone older.

6. *Guarding Privacy*

Young sisters should guard the privacy of their marriage. They should not divulge the intimacies of it unless they need help. Then husband and wife together should choose their counselor carefully.

A young, unmarried sister sometimes develops a very close relationship with another young sister with whom she shares many secrets. Whether this is wise could be questioned. Such relationships can become too intimate. At any rate, this relationship ends at marriage. The friendship may remain intact but at a completely different level. This change of loyalty should already be taking place during courtship. Things that she formerly shared with her close friend, she should learn to share with the one she hopes to spend her life with.

Sisters can enjoy good relationships when they observe Christian love, proper reserve, and respect for all. May God grant our sisters wisdom and grace to maintain wholesome relationships.

### F. Brethren and Sisters

"Rebuke not an elder, but intreat him as a father; and the younger men as brethren; the elder women as mothers; the younger as sisters, with all purity" (1 Timothy 5:1, 2).

This passage strikes a good balance on relationships between men and women. It promotes friendly regard on one hand and respectful reserve on the other. It balances the expressions "as mothers" and "as sisters" with the expression "with all purity." Actually, the two not only balance each other but also work together. A friendly regard between men and women calls forth reserve and respect. It is Christian charity at its best.

Christian men and women need each other in ways they do not always realize. Voluntary service units have included both men and women among their personnel in order to promote a family atmosphere. Church services normally include both men and women, and never is it more obvious that both are needed than during singing. Soprano, alto, tenor, bass—all blend their voices together.

However, the more valuable anything is to us, the more dangerous it is liable to be. For instance, the most valuable—and the most dangerous—relationship between adults is marriage. Either spouse can ruin the life of the other if he chooses to do so. Relationships between men and women not married to each other have fewer dangers, but dangers nonetheless. That is our subject in this section.

God created men and women with an attraction to each other. For this reason everyone must guard his own heart as he relates to anyone he is not married to. There is a pure way for men and women to relate to each other, and there is an impure way. Christians can know when they cross the line, but if they are not prudent, the line becomes blurry. The term "with all purity" indicates that we must exercise great carefulness. Special arrangements need to be made when men and women work together. We have various publishing houses that employ both men and women—married men as well as unmarried men and women. We employ men and women as co-teachers in our schools. Men and women work closely in some mission projects. Frequently we have young men or young women in our homes that are not of our families. These situations all require attention to maintaining pure relationships. We must not only make sure things *look* right; we must make sure they *are* right.

*1. Proper Greetings*

"Now concerning the things whereof ye wrote unto me: It is good for a man not to touch a woman" (1 Corinthians 7:1). The word *touch* calls for qualification. Most of us would agree that we can shake hands in all purity. But other touches are more significant. For example, if a man takes a woman's hand between his hands or rubs her arm a bit, he has crossed the line of Christian propriety and is outside the standard of "all purity."

Missionaries who work in other cultures need to learn how to handle the common greetings in those lands. In some Hispanic cultures, for instance, the common greeting involves much closer contact than we Americans are accustomed to. They take each other by the arm or even place one hand on the other person's shoulder. This way of greeting, even between men and women, takes us aback because of the way we were trained. It is not long until they learn that we do not appreciate that type of greeting and are satisfied with a handshake. If we are ever caught in such an experience, we need not feel guilty, but we should feel uncomfortable. At the same time, we need to be careful not to wrongly judge others who, in light of their culture, deem what they do to be perfectly appropriate.

*2. Dealing With Lust*

Jesus condemned looking on a woman to lust after her (Matthew 5:28). By nature, men do this very thing. Women by nature dress in a way that causes men to lust after them. This also is sin. For this reason the Bible commands women to dress modestly.

This matter is so serious that Jesus commands us to pluck out the eye that offends us. In practical terms, if we find ourselves in a situation where temptations continually confront us, we must leave. We must quit our job, change our location, or do whatever is necessary to escape the temptation. We do not need to feed our lusts; we can crucify them.

One man and one woman should never work alone together for any length of time unless, of course, they are married to each other. A minister should avoid being alone when he talks with a woman. He must especially beware of the woman who needs a lot of counseling. Are her motives pure? God does bring troubled women to Christian ministers, and there is a right way to help them. The minister's wife should be involved; she can be very helpful.

A married man's best defense is a good relationship with his wife. However, a happily married man should not assume that he is above temptation and become careless. He must always maintain a careful reserve. Men and women should not banter with each other. This breaks down reserve and opens the door for the wrong kind of exchange.

It is right, of course, for men to respect women by opening the door and allowing them to go first, by giving them their seat if someone needs to stand, or by giving a helping hand when it is needed. Society's effort to obliterate femininity is sinful. The feminine role is God honoring. Men should treat women with respect, honor, and civility. This is done without flirting.

We said that a married man's best defense is a good relationship with his wife. Actually, we all know that any man's *very* best defense, single or married, is a good relationship with the Lord. If he loves the Lord, he will take fair warning from the Lord's words that follow:

"But every man is tempted, when he is drawn away of his own lust, and enticed. Then when lust hath conceived, it bringeth forth sin: and sin, when it is finished, bringeth forth death" (James 1:14, 15). The Lord also promises that He "will with the temptation also make a way to escape, that ye may be able to bear it" (1 Corinthians 10:13). We can seek that escape and flee the temptation, or we can follow our lusts and die spiritually.

"Flee fornication. Every sin that a man doeth is without the body; but he that committeth fornication sinneth against his own body" (1 Corinthians 6:18). Many diseases are transmitted between individuals who disregard God's laws regarding purity. It is one of God's ways of punishing evil. The devil also transmits many spiritual diseases to Christians who do not commit fornication but nevertheless fail to keep their hearts pure.

*3. The Pure Way*

Thank God, there is a pure way for Christian men and women to relate to each other. Men and women can work together and complement each other. Women are better suited for some types of work, such as teaching little children. In mission work, single sisters can visit other women more appropriately than can a man. Many things can be done by both men and women in publishing houses without working too closely with each other. Christian propriety demands attention to dress, talk, posture, and thoughts. With high standards of conduct and the power of the Holy Spirit, we can maintain holiness and purity.

*4. Christian Courtship*

Single young men and women naturally enjoy each other's presence. At some point, many of them choose a special friend and begin courtship. In the world, courtship is for personal pleasure. But for the Christian it has a serious purpose—seeking a life companion.

Courtship requires more conscious reserve than normal life does. During courtship, a man and woman relate closely to each other, yet they must maintain reserve. When a man touches a woman, he arouses emotions that are right only within the marriage bond. For that reason, Christian courting couples maintain a "hands off policy."

A couple might take sinful liberties without committing actual fornication. But when they take liberties that arouse passions, they remove themselves from God's protection. They are relating to each other on a carnal level that makes it difficult, if not impossible, to make wise decisions. This could be tragic, because courtship sets the tone for marriage. It affords precious memories or lasting regrets. After marriage, some couples wonder why they did not understand such things during courtship.

The best way to "flee fornication" is for both young people to love the Lord more than they love each other. Their commitment to the Lord will keep them safe as long as they honor that commitment.

Once that is settled, Christian couples are free to devote their time to discovering each other's spiritual stature. They are in a position to intelligently discuss their ideals regarding money matters, church life, families, and children. They can discuss their likes and dislikes. They can discover at least some of the adjustments they will need to make if they marry.

Age, maturity, and parental involvement determine the frequency of a couple's visits. Just as courtship itself should be neither hasty nor unduly long, visits should not be either. Since long periods together bring temptations, long trips should be avoided. It is not necessarily wholesome for a couple to attend every wedding to which they are invited if they receive numerous invitations. Courtship is not for a couple to see how often they can be together, but rather to discover God's will. This can be done best when they are apart with time to reflect on what they know about each other.

## G. Youth to the Aged

"Thou shalt rise up before the hoary head, and honour the face of the old man, and fear thy God: I am the LORD" (Leviticus 19:32). "Rebuke not an elder, but intreat him as a father" (1 Timothy 5:1). "Let the elders that rule well be counted worthy of double honour, especially they who labour in the word and doctrine" (1 Timothy 5:17).

We generally think that the word *elder* refers to leaders. This is correct. It also refers to older men in general; all older men are leaders in one way or another. If nothing else, they are leaders of their own families.

This command to honor the aged is not only for young people, but it does include them. They should love old people and appreciate their contribution. They should resist the temptation to regard as outdated the ideas of older ones. Many youth could save themselves grief if they would seek advice from a grandparent or another older person.

If youth can speak disrespectfully of older people, it reveals a serious spiritual condition. Old people do develop foibles that can be quite amusing. We may rightly smile at them, but it is wrong to make fun of such weaknesses. One response represents acceptance and respect; the other, rejection. The difference is quite serious.

After all, old people know how we feel about them. We convey acceptance or rejection almost without saying a word. For that reason we cannot treat them properly unless we feel right about them.

God promises that it will be well with us if we honor our father and our mother. If youth extend that honor to their grandparents, it will be doubly well with them. God knows how we feel about our parents, and He knows how we feel about our grandparents. He blesses and uses young people who honor older people.

## H. Relating to the Handicapped and the "Different"

"For who maketh thee to differ from another? and what hast thou that thou didst not receive? now if thou didst receive it, why dost thou glory, as if thou hadst not received it?" (1 Corinthians 4:7).

"Blessed are the merciful: for they shall obtain mercy" (Matthew 5:7).

"He that oppresseth the poor reproacheth his Maker: but he that honoureth him hath mercy on the poor" (Proverbs 14:31).

*1. God's Plan*

The questions that Paul asked the Corinthians, we must ask ourselves. We are all different from each other. Why? Because God made us different. We sometimes forget this. We like to think that our traits make us just a little better than other people. Or we fall into the opposite trap—we fear that our oddity makes us inferior. This fear tempts

## Relationships That Bless

us to do things to prove that we are not inferior.

Unfortunately, not all Christians relate properly to others who are different from themselves. Those who are very handicapped may elicit compassion from us. But if someone is only slightly limited, we may be tempted to smile that knowing smile or even make an unkind remark. This is sinful because we are forgetting who gives us the capacities we have. The ability to work with dexterity comes from God. The other person's lesser ability also comes from God. God has decided whether we get five talents, two talents, or only one.

The other person's lesser ability gives us opportunities we would not otherwise have. It gives us a chance to serve and to learn humility. It is a sign of true greatness for someone to see those opportunities and stoop to help the needy.

When George Washington was general, he came upon a group of soldiers trying to move a big log. A corporal was off to the side shouting orders. General Washington stopped his horse and got down with the men. He then said, "All together, heave." The log slid into place. As he mounted his horse, he said to the corporal, "The next time you need something done, call on the general."

Jesus exemplified true greatness when He stooped to wash the disciples' feet. Nothing helps us more to maintain good relationships with the less fortunate than true Christlike humility.

Do not stare at the handicapped. Go talk to them. Smile and pat them on the shoulder. Even though they may not be able to respond to you, they know that you have taken time for them. At the same time let them minister to you by helping you be thankful for the good faculties you have.

Seek ways to help families with special children. Share with them in material ways when they have a financial burden. If at all possible, give the family a break. Take care of the special child for a day. "Bear ye one another's burdens, and so fulfil the law of Christ" (Galatians 6:2). Commend the family for the good care they are giving their child. They need to know that not only God but people also see their sacrificial love.

2. *Condescending or Condescended*

Encourage those who seemingly have but one talent. Commend them for what they can do well. Watch for opportunities to show them how you benefit by knowing them. This is the way to "condescend to men of low estate" (Romans 12:16).

There is a great difference between one who condescends and one who is condescending. The one who condescends puts himself on your level and makes you feel comfortable. Somehow he makes you feel that he never was above you. The condescending one maintains the feeling of aloofness. He keeps you aware that he is coming down to you; you always sense that he is above you.

An experience in Jesus' life illustrates this in Luke 7:36–50. Simon invited Jesus into his house. No doubt he thought he was honoring Christ by the invitation. As the sinful woman began her ceremony on the feet of Jesus, Simon mentally held himself above Jesus. "This man, if he were a prophet, would have known who and what manner of woman this is that toucheth him: for she is a sinner." Jesus truly condescended to the woman, whereas Simon was condescending.

We are by nature like Simon. We easily see ways in which others rate below us, and we tend to relate to them on that basis. But we must realize that we are what we are because of the goodness and kindness of God. This puts us on common ground with all others.

Jesus, for all His highness, was lowly, and "the common people heard him gladly" (Mark 12:37). They felt accepted. Jesus' followers today are the same. They can relate to anyone on any level in any culture.

The apostle Paul gave his testimony on this matter in 1 Corinthians 9:19–23. He began this passage by saying, "For though I be free from all men, yet have I made myself servant unto all, that I might gain the more." Those Christians who maintain that servant concept find it easy to relate to those who are limited in their abilities.

Finally, the Lord is watching, and we will let Him have the last word. "Inasmuch as ye have done it unto one of the least of these my brethren, ye have done it unto me" (Matthew 25:40).

*Chapter Four*

## *Relationships Within the School*

### A. School: A Tool for God

"Go ye therefore, and teach all nations," Jesus commanded His disciples, "teaching them to observe all things whatsoever I have commanded you" (Matthew 28:19, 20). Missionaries use this text, but the founders of schools may use it too. What better way is there to teach "all things" than for every church to have a school devoted to teaching children the truth?

The Christian school has been an integral part of the church throughout church history. Its prominence has risen and fallen in proportion to the spiritual temperature of God's people. The early Anabaptists revived Christian education when they taught the common people to read. Much more recently, the Christian day school movement again revived Christian education. Both of these revivals resulted from a deep respect for learning.

Teaching children about God and His truth is a privilege that many take for granted. It was not always this way. The devil has used many ways to take nations, churches, and cultures into the darkness of ignorance. He has done it in our own generation by having schools teach deceptive theories instead of truth. The success of error makes the efforts of the Christian school of great importance.

*Relationships That Bless*

The Christian school involves many people. Children come together and learn that children in other homes do things differently. In this respect, the church school has an advantage over the homeschool. It gives children the opportunity to learn to relate to other children. But they only profit from this when all the people involved learn to relate to each other in a Christian manner.

Several basic concepts come to our attention.

*1. The Value of Human Variety*

Basic to good relationships anywhere and especially in the school is this: God loves variety. "One star differeth from another star in glory" (1 Corinthians 15:41). On the same principle, God has made no two people exactly alike, not even identical twins. This infinite variety should intrigue us and cause us to accept each other. Instead, alas, it often causes conflict, pride, resentment, bigotry, and snobbery. Not only do these attitudes sever friendships, they are sin and must be repented of. People different from us can be a great blessing to us. Let us not lose that blessing.

*2. The Fact of Human Equality*

Most of us are afflicted with the idea that the more gifted a person is, the more important he is to God. Teachers and parents often tend to favor the brilliant child more than the one who struggles along. This is very unfortunate for all, especially for the slow child. Many times such a child misbehaves to gain acceptance or to distinguish himself or simply to get the attention of his peers.

Who said God needs gifted men and women to carry on His work? God has no need. If He had need, He could not be God. God can do anything. He uses man to do things, but He does not need man.

God created man not so much to be a servant as to be a worshiper, and anyone can worship. The man with one talent can be just as God honoring as the man with five talents. The little child who believes in God is just as God honoring as the eighty-year-old who continues to believe in God after a life full of tests and trials.

In fact, God delights in lowly things, not in things highly esteemed

## Relationships Within the School

among men. "But God hath chosen the foolish things of the world to confound the wise; and God hath chosen the weak things of the world to confound the things which are mighty; and base things of the world, and things which are despised, hath God chosen, yea, and things which are not, to bring to nought things that are: that no flesh should glory in his presence" (1 Corinthians 1:27–29).

We will relate to others best if we simply think of them as people God has chosen. This puts us on the same level with them.

*3. The Strength and Vulnerability of Groups*

One strength of church schools is that the various families can learn from each other's strengths and weaknesses. Probably most homes, including yours and mine, have a weak point that can be helped by other families who are strong on that point.

The mixture of children from various families can also create a weakness. One family of improperly trained children can cause problems and be a bad influence for the rest. In fact, any school can become a hotbed for corruption.

On the other hand, if only one family is unstable, the children from other homes can help them to learn better ways. This can work if those from well-ordered homes refuse to be impressed by erring conduct. Parents should make sure their children are not being led astray, and leaders should make sure the parents solidly support proper order and discipline in the school.

Even among sincere and sensible people, relationship problems surface. Often it is not in spite of, but because of these experiences that they learn the value of love, respect, and proper esteem for others.

In this chapter we will consider various ways to relate to each other in the school in order to maintain wholesome relationships.

## B. Parents to Teachers

We, the parents, hold the key for our children to have good relationships with their teacher. If we speak well of the teacher, our children will probably appreciate the teacher. If we drop a few remarks reflecting the incompetence of the teacher, our children will be quick to pick them up and share them with other children. When this takes place, the teacher is handicapped. Any teacher will function much better when he has the support of all the parents.

*1. Words Fitly Spoken*

As parents, we will need to use great care in what we say, how we say it, and to whom we say it. James, in speaking on this matter, said, "Behold, how great a matter a little fire kindleth!" (James 3:5). One uncontrolled tongue and a few undiscerning listeners can quickly create chaotic conditions. By contrast, in a spiritual brotherhood, a discerning parent may ask a few questions that change the whole perspective. You remember how Jesus did this. When the ruler of the synagogue reprimanded people for coming and being healed on the Sabbath day, Jesus asked, "Doth not each one of you on the sabbath loose his ox or his ass from the stall, and lead him away to watering? And ought not this woman, being a daughter of Abraham, whom Satan hath bound, lo, these eighteen years, be loosed from this bond on the sabbath day?" (See Luke 13:10–16.) With two questions, Jesus showed that He had done no wrong.

We can do the same. When someone gossips about the failure of a teacher or another home, we should help him turn his attention to his own need. This needs to be done in love.

School-age children know the weaknesses of their parents. They are quick to capitalize on them. They know whether they can get their parents to think negatively about the teacher. They also know if it is wise to keep quiet about any problems they may be having at school. They know whether or not their parents will support the teacher. We do ourselves and our children a great disfavor if we allow them to make negative comments about the teacher.

*2. Accepting Our Own Need*

We parents are often quite solicitous about our children, perhaps for our own sakes. We know that any problem our child may have in school could be blamed on parental failure. Usually we are slow to accept such blame. We would much rather blame the teacher. After all, teachers are not perfect.

But neither are parents, much less children. Rather than trying to place blame, we should consider what we can do to eliminate or at least minimize the problem. We must recognize that our child may need some help, especially if it is an individual problem.

In training our children, we need the observations of others. Obviously, we do not need interference, but we do need help. Children can become very adept at fooling their parents, and teachers may help to reverse this in our families by pointing out things we should know. Sometimes we would rather not know them. But if we refuse to face a need in the life of our school child, we will face it later when it will be much more difficult to deal with.

Pay attention to report cards. An understanding parent usually does not need an explanation for the marks that reflect on the character of the child. Still, it may be well to have the child tell you why he has the marks he does. Point out to him that some of the needs he has shown at school are showing at home too.

If you do not understand how your child could possibly have received the marks he did, consider the possibility that you as parents have been a little blind. Maybe some things are not important to you that should be. Most homes have some deficiencies. Do not be too proud to admit that yours may have some too.

*3. The Teacher, Our Friend*

Make teachers your close friends. Think of teachers as those who have your best interests at heart. They want to be successful teachers, and they want you to be successful parents. They are not competing with you.

A good relationship will develop with a teacher when parents express this thought: "We have tried to prepare this child for school, but we know he has much to learn. We are counting on you to help us. Not that you must do all we failed to do, but where our failures surface in school, we want to know about them so that together we can help the child develop properly. Please feel free to share with us."

Once you have laid the groundwork for a good working relationship, keep in touch with the teacher. This does not always have to involve troubleshooting. Social contacts, large and small, are in order.

*4. Dealing With Teacher Faults*

Sometimes teachers have serious faults. These should be brought to the attention of the board. If the school board does not see them as serious faults, do not cling to your evaluations. You may be biased in a wrong way. If, on the other hand, there are serious faults, do not make them worse by gossip or slander. Pray and give supportive encouragement. Express confidence in the teacher's basic integrity. This helps to maintain the needed working relationship.

What is a serious fault? If a teacher is partial to certain pupils, this is serious and will need attention. If someone has wanted to be a teacher but shows in the classroom that he is not qualified, this also is serious. Such a teacher should be replaced unless the board can give him effective help. Maybe a person is a capable teacher but is lazy and cuts corners. For instance, he might not keep up with his grading. Probably if the board gives the right kind of encouragement and supervision, such a teacher will become more diligent in his work.

*5. Handling Stories From School*

What about a story your child brings home that makes the teacher look bad? Throw a question mark over it immediately. You might test the child by telling him that you would like to check the story out. It may be that the child will begin to change some details in the story. Many times the child is simply wanting to see where your loyalties lie. Our children should discover early that we will not believe something simply because they say it.

It seems there was a teacher who sent a child home with a note running like this: "I promise not to believe everything your child says about home if you will do the same when he tells stories about school." Some children try to see how gullible we adults are. Yet they expect us to be wise enough to discern between truth and fantasy. Let us not disappoint them. Tales from school go home to more than one set of parents. What do we do when we are tempted to talk to another parent about a disappointing experience at school? What do we do when some other parent shares with us a tale of woe about the teacher? At such a point we hold the key to maintaining good relations or destroying them. Just realizing we are at a critical point might help us to say the right thing. If we blunder on without thinking, we might add fuel to an already destructive fire.

## C. School Board to Teacher

When it comes to setting the tone of the school, the board holds a strategic place. How do you as a board member feel about the teacher you hire? Do you think he is capable of handling a classroom well? The school board conveys trust or doubt to teacher, parents, and children. This in turn helps or handicaps the teacher, for people quickly pick up the attitudes of others, especially the attitudes of board members.

We would all prefer to hire only the best teachers, but this is not always possible. If you are approaching the beginning of the school year and do not have all the teachers you need, you may need to be satisfied with someone you consider less than ideal. However, God is able to use such a teacher if he is surrendered to the Lord and wants to learn. While you might be quicker than usual to give the teacher advice and direction, try to be as slow as always to question the teacher's attitude.

Besides, you might be pleasantly surprised. The fact that you found a teacher at the last minute does not mean that he will not be competent. Expect God to supply your school's needs.

*1. God's Blessing on the School*

Our Christian schools are miracles of God's grace and power. Generally, our teachers do a marvelous job. Our children have many reasons to be better prepared to face life than their contemporaries in the world. The united efforts of the Christian home and school give children a good foundation for life.

The success of the Christian school is not the result of the wise planning and management of men. It is the work of God. We must always see it as such. It is true that we have a part to do. We must continually apply our intelligence to the work. But since we see it as the work of God, we wait on Him for His wisdom and direction. If we indulge in self-congratulatory thoughts for our successful management of a school, we are headed for trouble. "God resisteth the proud, and giveth grace to the humble" (1 Peter 5:5).

*2. The Humble School Board*

Humility not only is right; it also has advantages. For one thing, it makes us approachable. People feel comfortable when they talk to us, and they also feel comfortable when we talk to them. They know we are free from suspicions, critical attitudes, and arrogant behavior.

Humility also helps us face issues objectively because self is out of the way. Our emotions or prejudices do not rule us. In any decision, we consider not only what we ourselves want, but what is for the overall good of the families involved.

*3. The Discerning School Board*

When teachers have ideas that they want to implement in the classroom, the school board must be discerning. The board can encourage personal initiative to a degree. But some teachers think the classroom is their own domain. It is, and yet it is not. Teachers are not self-employed; they are hired by the board, and they should do things in a way that is acceptable to the board.

An experienced teacher has mature ideas about how things should be done. The board should give latitude to a teacher who knows what works. Usually if a teacher has been successful in another school, a wise school board will allow the teacher freedoms as long as those freedoms do not violate the overall objectives of parents. But a good teacher will also know how to flex as he moves from one school to another.

A school board that needs to redirect a teacher should consider how to do this without making the teacher feel like a failure. What in the teacher is worthy of commendation? Did you hear a parent comment favorably about the teacher's performance? Have your children spoken favorably of the teacher? Let the teacher know that the parents are basically happy with his performance.

Ease into the matter with a question or a suggestion. For example, suppose the teacher does not spend enough time with the children at recess. As a rule, teachers should not leave children on the playground unsupervised. You may ask the teacher how often he finds it necessary to remain in the classroom when children are out at recess. You may suggest ways to avoid this. Maybe you know of things that happened at recess when the teacher was not present. You could mention that students prefer having the teacher present to maintain order and to keep the assertive students from controlling things.

If you are happy with the teacher's overall performance, you can convey criticism in a way that leaves the teacher feeling glad for your help. If you are mentally questioning the ability of the teacher, you will not convey confidence, and it may cause the teacher to also question his own ability. This damages relationships and hinders teaching.

*4. Relating to Individual Personalities*

Teachers' personalities vary greatly. Some are quite forward and free to say what they think. They ask questions and are very open about what goes on in school. Others are quiet and have little to say. Even though they may feel quite free with children, they feel intimidated in the presence of board members. Some teachers are quite self-assured and take things for granted, while others would not do anything without knowing the mind of the school board.

The board needs to avoid making unfavorable comparisons between teachers. Each has his virtues and qualities. Learn to evaluate the overall effect of a teacher's work. Only confront a weakness when you know it will have an adverse effect on the school. Give latitude to teachers to function within the realm of their capacity. Do not form a mold so rigid that it destroys individual initiative.

Relationships work best when we accept people as they are and

*Relationships That Bless*

appreciate them for the contribution they make to us. Note the special things an individual teacher does. Commend him. The teacher who knows he is appreciated will be much freer and more effective than one who doubts his acceptance.

Be sure your praise is sincere. Hypocrisy cannot be covered for long. Teachers appreciate those who are honest and open. The Bible commands us to maintain "unfeigned love of the brethren" (1 Peter 1:22).

The school board has the opportunity to maintain good relationships in the school. You need the wisdom of God, but praise His Name, you can have it. With that wisdom you can be a blessing to all involved.

## D. Teacher to School Board

How should teachers think about the school board? Should they be afraid of them? Should they make sure they tell them everything? Should they try to keep some things from them? Are they friends or foes?

The school board is the teacher's friend. If you are a teacher, assume this until the board notifies you otherwise. They hired you for what they thought were good reasons. Many of them have children you are now teaching, and they have a vested interest in the classroom. They wish you the very best.

You need not oversell yourself to the board by calling undue attention to your successes. Neither should you sweep a mistake under the rug; simply admit it. Otherwise you might create a situation very difficult for the board to dispose of. Teachers who are known to love God and their work need not fear to admit failure on any particular point. We all make mistakes, and the school board as well as parents should forgive when we fail. If we acknowledge our humanness, everyone can be understanding and supportive.

*1. Keeping the School Board Responsible*

The school board takes responsibility for the overall function of the school. If something goes wrong, the board must correct the matter. "Tell the chairman first" is a good rule to follow. If he hears about it directly from you, it will be much better than if he hears of it from some other source.

This needs a bit of clarification. If a problem arises that teacher and parents can take care of between themselves, the board need not become involved. But if either side feels uneasy about confronting the other, or senses that he is too emotionally involved to say a thing right, the board chairman can serve as a go-between. (We are talking now about school issues and not about interpersonal relations outside the classroom, in which case Matthew 18 applies.)

Some teachers can turn an insignificant thing into something big. On the other hand, some teachers can ignore something serious as being insignificant. In some cases, sharing the matter with a fellow teacher can put the matter in perspective before the board becomes involved.

The school board has a historical knowledge of the school; at least they should have. They do not tell you everything they know when they hire you. This is wise. Each year things change. New students come in. Sometimes new families join the church. Old families learn new ways of relating to others. People change their attitudes. It would be unnecessary and unwise to burden a new teacher with too much information. You may ask questions, but it is probably best to discover for yourself what kind of students you have.

2. *Keeping Yourself Free*

Teachers serve best if they stay free from biases. Even if a board gives you the history of some problem student or family, accept it as an opportunity to show the love of Christ. Remember the little poem that says,

> He drew a circle that shut me out—
> Heretic, rebel, a thing to flout.
> But love and I had the wit to win:
> We drew a circle that took him in!
> —*Edwin Markham 1852–1940*

A teacher can easily formulate opinions and biases based on sketchy information. If you do this, you are not as fair as you should be. Even the information that some well-meaning board member may share with you can be dangerous. Stow it away without letting it determine your action or reaction. Try to maintain objectivity in your relationships. That is, be free from emotional attachments or prejudicial exclusions.

*3. The Transitory Nature of Schoolteaching*

Many teachers in our church schools are rather transient. They teach for a year or two, and then they get married or go to another school or quit for some other reason. New teachers, often with a new supply of inexperience, take their place.

On the other side, the school board also changes from year to year. The changes on the school board will not bring in total strangers, for the teacher knows the families supporting the school from which board members come. Then too, the teacher knows that the ministry is usually involved in all the school board meetings. They help to maintain a continuity that eliminates any drastic changes in policy. Still, the board will bring in fresh blood now and then.

All this means that sometimes the teacher will have a new idea that does not fit the old ideas of the board, or the board will have a new idea that does not fit the old ideas of the teacher. The teacher should be able to flex a bit in order to work along with the board. When the board hands down a decision he does not like, he must resist the temptation to sabotage it by making sure it does not work. He must be open to ideas other than his own and do his best with them.

Share your opinions with the school board, but if the board's final decision runs counter to what you thought, accept that decision and support it. You might have a better idea than the board does, but the best idea you can have is to cooperate with the board.

## E. Parents to School Board

Everybody's business is nobody's business. For that reason we (the brotherhood) assign responsibility to a few men to see that what needs to be done gets done. When we delegate responsibility, we must give the delegates freedom to work within a certain boundary. That boundary is set by the brotherhood and not by certain parents. This requires all who send children to a school to be committed to supporting the decisions of the school board.

Of course there are many different ways to handle matters. Looking on, we can be sure that some things were not handled the way they should have been. But usually we do not have enough facts to make that kind of judgment. If we consider the value of good working relationships, we will avoid making hasty judgments that reflect on the competence of the school board.

The school board needs to hear from parents, especially wise parents, who will not take stories from their children at face value. Many stories that children bring home can be dismissed with an "I see; well, you make sure you behave yourself." However, sometimes parents will investigate a matter further, and if it does appear to be of a serious nature, they will bring it to the attention of the board. They should be careful not to present the matter as fact but rather as something that should be checked out. They should maintain a question in their own minds about the truth of the story.

Parents should remember that the board wants the best for everyone's children. They cannot make decisions based on one family's ideas. If an issue arises that causes polarization among parents, the school board must seek a right way. This requires wisdom, and someone is sure to be disappointed unless parents understand the value of maintaining harmony.

Once a young father was chosen to be chairman of the school board. The weight of the responsibility was extra heavy because patrons disagreed over the curriculum. Parents were becoming vocal and were polarizing. This young chairman knew the issue would need to be confronted, but he did not know how to bring the factions together. After praying about the matter, he finally called a meeting of all the parents and presented the issue.

Arguments came from both sides. Tensions mounted as the discussion heated. The chairman, feeling that things were getting out of control, broke down and wept. His wife began praying earnestly for her husband. The people soon quieted. The young man gained control of his emotions and pled with the people to try to work together rather than against each other.

Then the atmosphere of the meeting changed, and the people did just that. Each side began making concessions, and by the end of the meeting, they were all cheerfully accepting each other. What would have happened if the young chairman had promoted his own agenda? What would have happened if the chairman had decided to favor the one side? What would have happened if one family had insisted that a decision be made a certain way?

Remember that good relationships are more important than having your own way. If you put yourself in conflict with your brethren, pause to make sure the cause is God's and not your own. If the cause is God's, He really does not need you to defend it. You can state what you think and allow God to implement it. When you feel compelled to use pressure, you are giving others reason to feel that the matter is personal. That creates conflict.

Keep yourself in the love of God, and as a rule you will enjoy good relationships with your brethren.

## F. School Board to Parents

The board has no small task. They need to consider many factors as they face issues. They cannot simply favor those who are the most outspoken. Neither can they shield someone who needs redirection. They need to take into consideration the feelings and thinking of all the parents. Yet each family is an individual entity, and the board will want to meet the needs of each family.

For example, some children have difficulty learning while others gain knowledge without effort. The board should be careful not to criticize parents for having a slow learner. Granted, a child may be spoiled. Parents do fail. But critics are often too free with their opinions. Some parents spend hours trying to help their children, only to have onlookers say they are not diligent enough. The board will endeavor to gain reliable information on any matter to be discussed and not go by hearsay.

For another example, the board needs to be compassionate and long-suffering toward those parents who have trouble maintaining neat and orderly lives. Those who are naturally orderly and structured in their approach to life find it difficult to understand why others cannot be that way. I worked with a man once whose every move counted. We each had our own tools. He always placed the tools he used at the same place and never needed to look for them when he needed them. I was not that structured. I tried to follow his example, but invariably I would have to look around on my worktable to find certain tools. He might not have worked as fast as I, but his work was always done better than mine. I admired his ability, but I could not be like him, because God made me differently. I needed to learn what I could from him, but I could not change my basic format.

At the same time, the board needs to support a teacher's efforts to help a child improve. No child should say, "I know my desk is a mess, but that is just the way I am." School involves improving people's behavior, and the matter of orderliness should be no exception.

Variation in human ability provides a seedbed for jealousy, pride, or contempt. But it also provides a great opportunity—the opportunity to show the love of Christ. That supernatural love bridges gaps and breaks down barriers. Oh, that more would discover the great power of that love!

While everyone must be treated as an individual, everyone must be treated as normally as possible. Parents who think they are different think their children need special treatment. Do what you can to help these people think of themselves as normal. We are all different from each other, but that does not make us abnormal. We all have the same basic needs. There may be a variation in the extent of those needs, but they are needs just the same. We all need to be saved from sin. We all need to be loved, accepted, respected, and valued.

When the need for love and acceptance is not supplied, people turn to strange behavior, hoping to elicit the needed attention. This is not too uncommon among children, but it is perplexing when the unseemly behavior comes from parents. This type of disorder develops from years of wrong thinking. The school board should not try to deal with this problem alone; it requires ministerial help.

A lady interested in the Christian community was invited to spend a weekend with one of its families. Early in the introduction, her hosts told her she would find them quite different from run-of-the-mill Mennonites. They must have been right—the lady did not survive the whole weekend. She left early Sunday morning. The family did have ways that set them apart from their brethren, but the real problem was that they accentuated their differences. Such an attitude can also cause problems for our children in school.

The Christian school gives the brotherhood an insight into the homes of their brethren. We discover what kind of parents we are when we begin sending children to school. It is a place where we make comparisons. It gives parents an opportunity to make some changes before it is too late.

This applies to the school board as well. Board members usually have children in school. This requires carefulness and fairness on their part. They do not need to feel intimidated because their children are not perfect. They should simply do what they expect others to do—admit their problems and make the necessary changes.

The members of the school board along with the ministry have many opportunities to build good relationships, or to destroy them. If we remain humble and continually rely on the wisdom of God, we can be all that God wants us to be.

## G. Teacher to Pupils

How should teachers relate to their pupils? Should they remain aloof? Should they be stern and strict? Should they be loose and accommodating? Should they be buddies with the children? What is a good teacher?

Thankfully, there are only a few requirements. A good teacher loves

God with all his heart, loves children dearly, enjoys imparting knowledge, and reaches out for counsel. These are the basics; now for some practical observations.

## 1. Cultivating Good Relationships

Teachers rightfully want a warm, open, friendly relationship with their students. They establish this by taking a personal interest in each child. They listen to the stories their students have to tell. They sympathize with their students as they relate tales of woe. They laugh when their students share humor from home. They kindly coach their students in their struggles. They exercise discipline when their students cross boundaries. They stay involved with their students the whole time they are at school, including recesses and lunch hour.

Teacher–pupil relationships change drastically from grades 1 to 8. Peer pressure becomes a powerful influence over the adolescent. A wise teacher will not see this as competition. Rather he will try with God's help to maintain a heavy influence over the peer group. He will concentrate on an overall influence rather than a one-to-one relationship. If he keeps the goodwill of the group, peer pressure will be in his favor.

Saying it another way, if the teacher keeps the atmosphere right, the occasional student who has a grumpy morning will find himself cheered by the good feelings of the other students. But if the teacher, by being disagreeable, spoils the atmosphere and alienates most of the students, the grumpy student will have difficulty snapping out of his negative attitude. He has too many comrades nearly as glum as he.

Occasionally there is an extremely insecure child in school. Many questions arise about such a child. Why is he insecure? Is it a personality weakness? Is it a home problem? We will deal with these questions in the next section. But you, teacher, may hold the key to helping such a child. Sometimes having a close relationship with his teacher will be just what he needs. But beware! Be sure you do not create a teacher's pet and cause him greater problems among his peers.

*2. Helping the Insecure*

An insecure student needs an understanding teacher. The first thing the teacher must understand is that insecurity is a broader problem than it appears to be and underlies problems that do not look like insecurity at all. A loudmouthed, pushy child might actually feel insecure. While dealing with such a child's difficult exterior to keep him from being too troublesome to others, the teacher should also try to deal with the root of the matter.

Regrettably, the root is often beyond a teacher's reach. Perhaps the child is not well accepted at home, or perhaps he was abused before he came to that home. Or perhaps both (God forbid). Perhaps he started school too young and developed immature habits that he has not shaken off. Perhaps he has perceptual difficulties that keep him from understanding what others understand at a glance. This can destroy confidence. (A middle-aged man once remarked about his boyhood, "I couldn't understand why everyone was laughing at me.")

If, however, the root of the child's problem is within your reach, do what you can. If he feels inadequate in his studies, maybe a little extra coaching from an older student would help. If he is being pushed around (by a bully who also feels insecure), take charge and put a stop to the mistreatment. If it is a home problem, alert the ministry if they do not already know about the problem.

In any case, keep a genial atmosphere. Not only love the child but also show it. Show it in little discreet ways, for insecure children do not always respond well to overt compliments. Draw a smile on the top of an assignment paper, or write an extra comment in red ink on a composition, or drop your hand on his desk as a friendly gesture. Pay attention when he has something to say.

Tim was an adopted child. His father died in a farm accident when Tim was small. His widowed mother tried her best, but there were real lacks in the home. He was the youngest and the only boy in the family, and he needed a father very much. He was difficult to get close to. In school he chose mischief to glean attention. I substituted for three weeks while he was in the upper grades.

One day when I was not able to be on the playground during recess, I did the unthinkable. I made him responsible to maintain order on the playground. I could see that it sent a message of trust to him that he had seldom experienced. The usually trusted students were aghast, of course. A couple of remarks escaped, suggesting that maybe I had slipped a cog or two. But all went well. If I had been a long-term teacher, I would not have done that every time, of course. But insecure children need to get the message that they are responsible and will be trusted with responsibility. With God's help, teachers can make a great difference in the lives of troubled children.

Be predictable. Nothing helps an insecure child like knowing what is going on. Stick to your rules; stick to your penalties; stick to your rewards. The insecure child will feel better about your rules than about the exceptions you make for him.

Govern the other children. Do not let them make fun of him. This will only increase his feelings of incompetence. If he shows off, encourage the other children to make him feel accepted in ways other than laughing at his antics.

The day may come when you will want to explain to the class how to be friends with the insecure child. This should be done when the child is absent. Be sure you do not reflect on the child in an unkind way. Rather, use that time to correct any wrong responses from the other children.

Interestingly, what the teacher and students do not do might be more important than what they do. When working with an insecure child, everyone must be matter-of-fact in their friendliness and must resist the temptation to play psychiatrist.

A bold, aggressive, self-asserting student presents a special challenge, especially in the upper grades. He often has skills in undercutting others. The teacher is his number one rival, since he is the authority. Such an individual can be difficult to love. Yet without love, especially disciplinary love, you will not win his respect. He must be made to understand that you are in authority—that he cannot run the show. If he cannot get the message any other way, he might need to be suspended for a time.

The most emotionally needy student might nevertheless be a natural leader with a flair for getting other children to do things his way. With his personal magnetism, he might urge others on in mischief, even getting them to do things he would not do himself. With God's wisdom, knowing how to be firm but gracious, you can steal the hearts of his comrades. If they discover that they cannot beat you, they will join you. Try to see insecure students as more than just a threat. The Lord is giving you the opportunity and the challenge to make a significant difference in their troubled lives.

*3. The Blessing of Variety*

The great variety of students that a teacher faces keeps him from becoming bored. This variety also requires a teacher to have a large, open heart, ready to accept each student that God gives him. Many students will go about their work without much supervision. While thanking God for these, the teacher should also thank God for those who do take more supervision. If he cannot thank God for some student, he will not treat that student properly. Sometimes a teacher may need to pray awhile before his heart is filled with love for the pupils who do not fit the pattern he likes. If that love is maintained, he will be an effective teacher.

## H. Teacher to Teacher

Many schools have two or more teachers. The smooth function of the school depends upon good relationships between the teachers. Every experienced teacher is a wealth of resource material for others. New teachers should respect the experience of others without feeling intimidated by their own inexperience. Older teachers should maintain a humble attitude about their experience. This helps new teachers feel at ease around them.

Actually, the more experience a teacher has, the more humble he should be. He should have discovered that he really has much more to learn. He should also know that what worked one time did not work

## Relationships Within the School

another time. For that reason he will be slow to say, "This is how you do it." An experienced teacher can often tell what did not work for him and let the younger teacher go from there. There will, however, be times when he must give positive direction.

### 1. The School Meeting Contribution

A school meeting is a very interesting place. Teachers discuss subjects from the standpoint of experience. They soon discover many different ways to handle matters. Sometimes new teachers leave those meetings feeling overwhelmed with ideas. They soon learn that they must go on being themselves even at the expense of some ideas they have heard. They can learn things from others, of course, but no two persons are alike, and no two situations are alike. Each teacher must consult with his own heart and with God to make applications that suit his own classroom.

### 2. Honesty About Feelings

"Where there are people, there are problems." Teachers are no exception. We all carry the potential to become jealous, to be suspicious, to imagine things, to be proud and snobbish, and to be hateful and unforgiving. Usually we deny that any of these feelings exist in our heart. We try to cover any traces of their outworking. But any wrong feelings in our heart will affect relationships. The only way to deal with these feelings is to be honest with God. Tell Him how it is. Tell Him why you have difficulty loving, and then tell Him that He will need to help you rid your heart of these bad feelings so you can love. God can work with that kind of honesty.

When people are honest with God, He has a way of bringing the searchlight around to focus on the evil of their own hearts. If we do not enjoy a good relationship with a fellow teacher and we deny any fault on our part, God cannot help us. However, He will help us if we are honest with Him about our true feelings. It does not sound very nice to say, "God, I hate Jane. She is so obnoxiously proud." That sounds like an awful thing to say to God because we know that he that hates his brother is a murderer at heart. But really, God knows you hate Jane. You will not be telling Him anything He did not know.

We like to hedge a bit. We like to think that we do not really hate Jane, but we just do not feel good toward her because of her objectionable character. But God always has a remedy for honest people. He forgives repentant murderers, but He will not forgive the persistent liar. If we ask God to forgive us for our hatred, we can then ask that God might forgive Jane for her obnoxious pride. Quite likely we will discover that it is our own obnoxious pride that makes us hate Jane. We fear that kind of discovery, but, oh, the peace and power that accompanies that kind of revelation!

*3. Proper Arrangements Between Teachers*

School boards should consider whether a working relationship is suitable. For instance, how will it be to have a young unmarried man and a young unmarried woman working together? Even married teachers need to consider propriety. In some schools the after-school schedule is arranged so that two people are not working there together for long periods of time.

Proper reserve can be maintained if both know what proper reserve is. Some people are naturally outgoing and friendly. A fellow teacher may consider this a lack of reserve. We need to be wary lest we accuse others of motives they do not have. If someone needs help understanding proper reserve, the school board should give that help. Better yet, a school board should take into consideration the personalities involved and provide satisfactory arrangements from the beginning of the school year.

Aside from these considerations, common friendships among teachers carry great potential. If you are a teacher, allow mutual regard to grow at a normal rate. Do not try to force it from the first day. Then again, do not stifle it by opinions you form before you even meet your co-teacher. Maybe you heard something negative about the community from which he comes. Maybe someone even gave you his opinion about him. You begin to envision what he will be like. You should avoid this as much as possible. You will discover for yourself what he is like.

Prejudice is never right and is very injurious to relationships.

Teachers, to be effective, must be interested in others. This interest must be not only in their students but also in people in general. This makes them much more resourceful in their teaching. I have watched with interest when two teachers get together. Ere long they are talking about school. I thrill to see their interest and dedication to their work.

None can calculate the value of the contribution these dedicated people have made to our homes and churches. We trust God will reward them for the sacrificial services they have rendered to His kingdom. The positive influences of our teachers are multiplied as they do their part in helping to maintain good relationships between each other and between brothers and sisters in the church.

*Chapter Five*

## *Relationships Within the Community*

"And now come I to thee; and these things I speak in the world, that they might have my joy fulfilled in themselves. I have given them thy word; and the world hath hated them, because they are not of the world, even as I am not of the world. I pray not that thou shouldest take them out of the world, but that thou shouldest keep them from the evil. They are not of the world, even as I am not of the world. Sanctify them through thy truth: thy word is truth. As thou hast sent me into the world, even so have I also sent them into the world" (John 17:13–18).

Several things in this passage immediately arrest our attention. First, the world hates the Christian. Next, this hatred comes because Christians take seriously the Word of God. Also, there is an obvious separation between the Christian and the world. In the midst of this tension between the Christian and the world, God gives the Christian His joy. This joy further antagonizes the world because they cannot understand how the Christian can be so happy when he has the whole world against him. Thus the tension remains as long as the Christian maintains his attachment to the Vine, Jesus Christ.

## A. Basic Principles

*1. Separated and Rejected*

Twice in the above verses, Jesus said of His followers, "They are not of the world." God made this division at the Fall of Man. God told the serpent, "I will put enmity between thee and the woman, and between thy seed and her seed" (Genesis 3:15). Since God put that enmity there, it will remain until Jesus comes.

Part of this enmity is kept alive because the Christian's work is to preach the Gospel—to share the Good News. We often think of this in terms of "winning souls" for Jesus. There is nothing wrong with this expression, but as a matter of strict fact, we do not win souls. We are responsible to present truth to people, but we cannot change the heart of another person. It is God who works in hearts and wins them to Himself.

People we meet do not realize this. As they accept or reject the Spirit's working in their hearts, they tend to accept or reject us personally. They may ignore us, thinking we are unbalanced. They may decide that we are dangerous persons who must be aggressively opposed. They may test the validity of our Christianity by doing things to provoke us to anger. Any of these responses from people causes our flesh to cringe.

Probably one of the greatest temptations we Christians face is that of trying to avoid the rejection of the world. We want neighbors to think well of us. We want businessmen to respect us. We hesitate to disturb others with the truth of the Gospel. As honorable as the quiet approach may seem to us, it is usually carnal. Not that we should deliberately try to antagonize people, but the Lord wants to knock on their heart's door whether they like it or not.

*2. Separated to Serve*

We Christians, by the new birth, become citizens of the heavenly kingdom. We become ambassadors for Christ in an alien country. In some ways this puts limits on what we can do. We observe various thou-shalt-nots that people of the world never think of observing. But something else is just as true, though we easily forget it. Being a separate people broadens our opportunities because it makes us universal. By being completely free from national pride, political agendas, and worldly ideologies, we can effectively go into all the world to preach the Gospel to every creature.

This does not come naturally. We carry with us the influences of our homes and communities. We are patriotic by nature. We tend to bristle when we hear someone speak reproachfully of our country or community. As Christians, we should learn to rise above that. The world is the same everywhere. Whether American, European, Asian, African, or Hispanic, every culture is ungodly. Hatred, patriotism, animosity, and bigotry are found everywhere. Therefore, the Gospel is needed everywhere, and our commitment to the Gospel makes us universal.

Christians grapple unnecessarily with the practical outworking of being part of a separate kingdom and yet meeting the needs of those about them. How, they wonder, can a person be a part of a kingdom so different and superior—"a chosen generation, a royal priesthood, an holy nation, a peculiar people" (1 Peter 2:9)—and yet effectively serve his earthly community? The fact is, being part of a separate kingdom is the key to effective service. Without being separate from society, what could we offer? Jesus was "separate from sinners" (Hebrews 7:26), yet He served the sinners about Him. Certain disciples were called "these that have turned the world upside down" (Acts 17:6). That was how they helped people the best.

*3. Separated to Be Ambassadors*

"Now then we are ambassadors for Christ, as though God did beseech you by us: we pray you in Christ's stead, be ye reconciled to God" (2 Corinthians 5:20). In what ways are we ambassadors?

An ambassador represents the country of which he is a citizen. He cannot be a citizen in the country where he lives. He cannot enter into the functions of the citizenry, such as voting or holding political office. It is a disgrace when a national ambassador becomes a traitor and begins to collaborate with the country to which he is sent. Jesus, ambassador for His Father, steered clear of Roman politics and pagan methods. It is likewise wrong for a Christian, an ambassador in Christ's stead, to enter into the political affairs of nations.

An ambassador's work is conciliatory. He tries to gain the goodwill of foreign citizens toward his own country. Christ did the same when He was here. He showed us the goodness and kindness of God. Through His work, many changed their thinking about God and were reconciled to Him. Today the Christian's work is to help God's enemies see that they are mistaken in their feelings toward God. A Christian rejoices when people begin to love God and serve Him instead of themselves.

To accomplish this, we adorn the doctrine of God before our neighbors. When our homes are full of happy relationships, the community knows it. When we manifest the fruit of the Spirit to the ungodly, the Spirit of God may awaken a thirst in their hearts to find the same peace and joy.

We of course do not try to impress people with our godly lives. Rather, we naturally reveal the living relationship we have with God. God's blessing and glory in our lives makes our relationship with Him attractive to others.

There is a sense, however, in which a national ambassador is different from a Christian. An ambassador tries to make peace between nations but does not encourage people of one nation to escape to another. We Christians do the opposite. The nations of the world will always be against the kingdom of Christ. We want to help citizens of this world get transferred to a new kingdom. We urge them to turn their allegiance from Satan to God. We cannot do this by negotiating alliances between the two kingdoms. Rather, we do it by maintaining a distinct separation.

*4. Separated Indeed*

It is possible to have a purely artificial separation between Christians and the world. This serves only to maintain a distinct culture. The Pharisees had that kind of separation. It served their purposes, but it did not advance the cause of God. Jesus did not upbraid them for their separation, but for their worldliness. They were humans—unconverted, self-righteous humans. Their type of separation served neither God nor man. It was selfish and self-centered, and it only served to maintain a system.

A beneficial separation from the world is brought about by the Spirit. Men and women governed by the Holy Spirit have a completely different motivation from worldlings for what they do, what they say, how they think, and how they appear. "Old things are passed away; behold, all things are become new" (2 Corinthians 5:17).

Everything about a Christian makes him a separated person. Lusts and carnal desires do not motivate him. His view of wealth, prestige, fame, and worldly acceptance is completely different from that of the unconverted. His humble demeanor marks him as a man set apart from the world.

His outstanding character often arouses interest in many onlookers. Some, of course, may be suspicious for a while, but usually in time they will trust him and wonder why this man is so different. This is according to God's plan, and blessed is the man who is ready to give Bible answers to the questions that come.

## B. Practical Applications

### 1. Learning to Give

What kind of social exchange do Christians have in the community? You cannot really have extensive involvement. It is always right, however, to be neighborly. Visit them and show interest in their spiritual understanding. Discuss the Lord and spiritual values with them. Be friendly but not chummy.

Help them in times of need or distress. If a family in the community suffers loss through a storm or fire, give them a hand. Visit them when they are sick or when they have a new baby. If they do you a favor, accept it graciously if you can. This helps to build relationships more than doing a favor for them.

Christians find fulfillment and satisfaction in the fellowship of brethren. This is as it should be. But sometimes we are too content in our quiet communities. We do not allow ourselves to become involved with the needs of others. The story of the Good Samaritan teaches us what it means to be a neighbor. It can be both demanding and costly. It probably means much more than we are willing to admit. The response of the priest and the Levite fits all too well the response of busy religious men today.

So easily we forget that if we get involved with people, we will enjoy it. God designed us this way. The Good Samaritan was likely able to enjoy satisfied sleep after his deed of kindness. The priest and the Levite probably felt uneasy.

Today the government has many programs to care for the poor. Churches too have agencies that reach out to the indigent. It is easy to salve our conscience by writing out sizable checks to these agencies. But this does not solve the problem next door. Jesus said, "For ye have the poor always with you" (Matthew 26:11).

Government programs cannot eliminate the poor. Some people do not know how to manage money. The more handouts they get, the more they need. In desperation, they waste money on lottery tickets, drugs, or alcohol. They need a caring heart, someone to show them the love of Jesus.

Can Jesus tap us on the shoulder and remind us of a need we know about? Can He say, "Go to such a place in town, and you know you will find someone who needs help"? Are we willing to pray and ask God to lead us to those who need His love? Do we see the divorced and remarried as anything other than hopeless cases? Do we have anything to say to someone whose loved one committed suicide? Are we willing to invest the time, money, and prayers it takes to rescue people from the welfare system?

We may think that with the welfare system and all our economic opportunities, there is no excuse for anyone to be poor. There may be no excuse, but there are reasons. God does not give everyone the ability to manage finances to an economic advantage. He sees to it that

## Relationships Within the Community

some of the world's poor live near us, and He notes how we relate to them.

One proof of Christ's authenticity was that He preached the Gospel to the poor" (Matthew 11:5). The poor continue to need the Gospel. They need salvation. Until we lead them to Jesus, we have not really helped them. Material aid is good, but it can cloud or overshadow spiritual matters.

2. *Learning to Receive*

According to Mathew 10 and Luke 10, Jesus sent out His disciples without silver or gold, without extra coats, and without extra food. They were to inquire after the worthies in a town and abide with them. They were to say, "Peace be to this house." While they evangelized in that town, they were to stay in the same house and eat what their hosts gave them. Thus they became dependent upon their hosts. This created a relationship from which both benefited.

Jesus was our example of supplying others' needs and also of depending on others. Once when He fed the multitude, He did it with a lad's lunch. He did not reach into His own pocket for it. How do you think the lad felt when it was over? Did he feel indebted to Christ? Do you suppose he felt cheated? No, for he had become a partner in the ministry of Jesus. The kingdom of Jesus is designed to have people interdependent. The success of the church depends on that interdependence.

How can we Christians help the poor without making them feel indebted to us? Sharing the Gospel with the poor does not put them under obligation to us but to God. If they respond to the Gospel, they will have a giving heart. Recognize the contribution they make to you or to the church. Let them do things for you; even ask them to do something for you. We naturally hate to bother them in this way, but really, this gives them a sense of worth.

Think of the difference Elijah made in the life of a widow. She was very near the end. She had one meal left when Elijah came. Of all things, he asked for that one meal. The Bible says that Elijah was subject to passions like ours. He was an ordinary man. But he served God, and it was not a disgrace to ask for a meal—the last that the woman had. With God's blessing, she lived a long time on that last bit of meal. That widow gave her last and helped herself in the process. It was an interdependent exchange.

Sometimes we hear people lamenting the loss of interworking relationships. Then they reminisce how they harvested together or shared tools or went visiting. Such sharing is invaluable. The selfish independence of our generation fits the description of the Laodicean church—they "have need of nothing" (Revelation 3:17). The end is spiritual and moral loss.

Let others do things for you. Ask them for a glass of water. When we recognize that we need each other—yes, even our ungodly neighbors—we all benefit.

*3. Learning to Be Impartial*

Relating to the rich in the community presents another kind of opportunity. We generally think of them as being hard to reach with the Gospel. Many may be; however, the rich have everything except what they really need. They do not have peace, joy, or real happiness. They need Jesus.

Although Jesus said that the rich shall hardly enter the kingdom of God, He did say that it is possible with God. As we pray and watch for opportunities to show the love of Christ, God can work to cause even the rich to seek salvation.

Zacchaeus was a rich man, but his wealth did not keep him from receiving Jesus joyfully. Note how Jesus approached him: "Zacchaeus, make haste, and come down; for to day I must abide at thy house" (Luke 19:5). Jesus did not say, "Zacchaeus, you need me." Rather He said, "*I must abide at thy house.*" Here again we see the interdependent relationship that Jesus maintained.

Although it is right to be interested in a rich man's salvation, James teaches us that it is wrong to favor a rich man that comes into our assemblies (James 2:1–9). He addresses the problem of respect of persons—despising the poor and favoring the rich. We are tempted to think that the soul of the rich man is more valuable than the soul of the poor. This of course is not true.

We should be slow to estimate a man's character by his financial standing. It may simply be a reflection of his God-given ability to manage his God-given possessions. Or it could be that he loves money and finds pleasure in gain at the expense of others. Regardless of how a man gains his wealth, God can touch his heart and expose any evils lurking there. In order to relate to him properly, we must let God work in his heart and avoid hastily judging him.

*4. Learning Self-forgetfulness*

"But sanctify the Lord God in your hearts: and be ready always to give an answer to every man that asketh you a reason of the hope that is in you with meekness and fear" (1 Peter 3:15). Why the fear? We fear lest people should see only us.

This happens. People become attracted to us for our way of living. They begin to look to us for guidance. We begin to explain to them why we do what we do. We begin to expound to them doctrine—without making sure they have been converted.

This invariably leads to disaster. Without the new birth, they do not find peace. They balk at some change required of them. In their rebellion, they begin to scrutinize our lives and discover weaknesses and failures. They turn bitter and become our enemies. We have failed to lead them beyond ourselves.

This type of problem occurs over and over in human relationships. Someone becomes attracted to an acquaintance by some seemingly exceptional virtue. He cultivates a friendship and carries high regard toward his friend for a while. Then something causes him to question his high opinion of the other, and the relationship deteriorates. Ere long more things pile up until he begins to despise the one he once regarded highly. What can we do to keep this from happening?

We can usually sense when others think too highly of us. We should confront them, stating it as it is: "You think too highly of me. I'm not the perfectly good person you think I am. You will soon discover that I am a man of like passions as you. I need Jesus every day to save me and forgive me just like you do."

In Acts 14:8–18, some people mistook Paul and Barnabas for gods in the likeness of men and prepared to worship them. Paul and Barnabas were greatly troubled and rent their clothes and forbade the people to think such things. Even though people today do not take it this far with us, the matter is still serious.

Besides telling them frankly that we are only human, we can commit the problem to the Lord. We can ask Him to bring circumstances to help people see us in a proper light. One bishop prayed to this effect, and shortly afterwards he accidentally spilled the glass of water on the pulpit. This was probably part of the Lord's answer.

Consider how Jesus handled the man who called Him "Good Master." Jesus said, "There is none good but . . . God" (Mark 10:17, 18). When we sense that people think too highly of us, we should somehow let them know that there is none good but God. The humble Christian not only thinks this way, he lives it. He speaks of God's goodness, grace, and power. He refuses to take any credit for goodness or virtue.

Could it be that we cannot lead people beyond ourselves because we are not humble enough? Are we content to have others think more highly of us than is just? If we think we are more qualified than others to help people spiritually, we will miserably fail. We cannot lead others to a faithful walk with the Lord Jesus if we have them attached to us.

Do you want good relationships with those around you? Follow Paul's advice: "I therefore, the prisoner of the Lord, beseech you that ye walk worthy of the vocation wherewith ye are called, with all lowliness and meekness, with longsuffering, forbearing one another in love; endeavouring to keep the unity of the Spirit in the bond of peace" (Ephesians 4:1–3).

*Chapter Six*

# Christian Employee and Employer Relationships

## A. Basic Principles

"Servants, be obedient to them that are your masters according to the flesh, with fear and trembling, in singleness of heart, as unto Christ; not with eyeservice, as menpleasers; but as the servants of Christ, doing the will of God from the heart; with good will doing service, as to the Lord, and not to men: knowing that whatsoever good thing any man doeth, the same shall he receive of the Lord, whether he be bond or free. And, ye masters, do the same things unto them, forbearing threatening: knowing that your Master also is in heaven; neither is there respect of persons with him" (Ephesians 6:5–9).

"Masters, give unto your servants that which is just and equal; knowing that ye also have a Master in heaven" (Colossians 4:1).

"Servants, obey in all things your masters according to the flesh; not with eyeservice, as menpleasers; but in singleness of heart, fearing God" (Colossians 3:22).

The master–servant relationship of New Testament times was not exactly the same as the employer–employee relationship of today. For example, in a free enterprise system, an employee may freely change from one employer to another without violating Scriptural principles. But the same basic principles that once governed servants and masters still apply in our time.

## B. The Christian Employer

No one has more bosses than the boss. He must not only please his customers, but he must also give due consideration to the wishes of his employees. More important, he must please his Master in heaven. The Lord holds controlling interest in the enterprise; in fact, He owns it all. This fact determines what an employer requires of his employees.

*1. Relating to Employee Needs*

A Christian employer often renders a worthwhile service to the public. He wants God to be magnified by the quality of his work. He wants customers to be satisfied and happy that he has done a very good job—well worth their money. If he hires employees, he wants each employee to be committed to the same principles of quality workmanship. Each employee must be concerned about the reputation of the business. Each must understand that what he does makes a difference.

Profit and job security may be acceptable motivations, but more important is the glory of God. Is this business the type that God can bless? If it only provides luxury items for an affluent society, Christ would say, "Seek ye first the kingdom of God" (Matthew 6:33). Assuming that the business produces something useful, the employer should expect his employees to dedicate themselves to their work. Only by putting their hearts into their work can they glorify God.

Should a Christian ever employ unbelievers or believers from other denominations? He can as long as his testimony is not hindered. Non-Christians can understand the value of quality work. Sometimes they can be very dedicated to their work. In fact, a Christian employer once said he would rather hire non-Mennonites than Mennonites because many of them are more dedicated to their job. They are not frequently asking to go to weddings or other social functions.

This raises another question. When is it legitimate for employees to have time off work? Some workers rather freely leave their work and go to whatever social function is beckoning. The affluence of our time frees them from the restraint of financial need. With lots of money or easy credit, they do not dedicate themselves to their work. This creates problems for employers. Granted, certain social functions are important. But God values labor too.

Christians need to work together to discern the will of God in these matters. Is the employer expecting too much dedication? Is the employee too careless in his attitude toward his work? When all involved want the will of God, the matter can be discussed without causing friction.

An employer has employees to consider, and he also has customers to satisfy—on time. As a result he can face some dilemmas. He will need to take time to walk with God to be sure that God is in control of both his life and his business.

*2. Relating to Differing Personalities*

Employees differ. Some are fast and some are slow. Some are diligent and some are lazy. Some are careful, and they tend to be slow. Those who work faster may need to do things over to get them right. Some like to visit on the job, whereas others ignore what is going on around them and stick to their work.

An employer needs to learn how to relate effectively and compassionately to each one. Certain personalities tend to provoke him, whereas others attract his favor. Each person needs to feel accepted. Although some need more supervision, the employer must give it in a way that maintains the self-respect of the individual. An employer may discover that one of his employees can do the coaching better than he can.

Since an employer needs to deal with a variety of employees, he may find it helpful to remember these questions Paul asks in 1 Corinthians 4:7: "For who maketh thee to differ from another? and what hast thou that thou didst not receive? now if thou didst receive it, why dost thou glory, as if thou hadst not received it?" God gives each one his personality, and an employer can learn to see value in each one. He can see others as equals or even esteem them better than himself (Philippians 2:3).

The variety among employees might turn to the employer's advantage. What one man does not think of, another one might. A wise employer can accept employees' suggestions for improving methods and quality.

## C. The Christian Employee

Blessed is the Christian employee who remembers that he is working for Jesus. "As unto Christ" and "as the servants of Christ" are principles that guide him. How easily he can forget that his Master is Jesus and begin to focus on a man, the employer. In that case he can soon develop wrong attitudes.

The principles that guide an employee are not numerous. They can easily be memorized. But they will not guide us unless we have the Spirit of God in our hearts. We will not be Christian in our conduct unless we walk with the Lord in all that we do. Let us take a look at the principles.

*1. The Christian Employee Is Obedient*

We carry opinions about many things. We have learned ways of working from our parents or from experience. We tend to think these ways are best. Nevertheless, "Be obedient to them that are your masters" applies just the same.

Sometimes when an employer asks us to do something, he explains how he wants it done. We may think we know of a better way to do it. We may think that he ought to be happy to have us choose the more efficient way, only to discover that he is not happy that we did not follow his instructions. Does he have a right to be troubled about something like this? Yes, he does. We have not been obedient.

At times we can discuss matters or give suggestions, but usually the best way is to quietly obey without question. If an employer says, "This is the way I generally do it, but maybe you know of a better way," then we have the opportunity to suggest another way.

I had the privilege of working with a man who had learned this lesson well. He and I were on a job together. The boss told us how he wanted a job done. I was young and full of "wise" ideas. I thought there was a better way—an easier way to do the job. I voiced my opinions to my fellow worker. He nicely told me that he did not care if it took us twice as long to do it the way the boss asked us to do it; he would do it that way. After all, the boss was paying us to work for him and not for our ideas. It was a valuable lesson that the Lord did not let me forget.

When an employee faithfully follows directions, he becomes a trusted man. Ere long he will be given greater responsibility with the privilege of making his own decisions. He will usually be allowed to do a job in whatever way he deems best.

Obedience in all things touches attitudes also. The man who likes his master loves to please him. He works with a gusto that often affects those around him. A truly Christian employee will be a happy man, for he loves his Master, Jesus. He has all heaven on his side. He has many promises of God to encourage him to always do right. He has the smile of God upon him.

Normally, a Christian employee should be able to promote his employer and his business. If the employer does things he cannot approve of, the employee should question his own motives first. "Am I free from jealousy? Do I really love my boss? Am I seeing beyond him to my accountability to Christ? Am I working for Jesus or for my employer?" The Bible does not tell the servant to judge the rightness of what his master does. There is a place for talking with an employer (especially a Christian one) if we believe he is doing something wrong, but only out of a heart of love.

In a free-labor market, we can change employers without violating Christian principles. But as long as we work for an employer, we are to be subject to him, even though he may be the froward type (1 Peter 2:18). If we develop a bad attitude toward an employer, we sin and must repent of that bad attitude. Changing employers will not free us of guilt.

## 2. The Christian Employee Is Faithful

"Not with eyeservice, as menpleasers" reminds the Christian who works diligently while the boss is around not to slack off when he leaves. He faithfully labors to give good measure in his time on the job. He is working for Jesus, and Jesus is worthy of the best all the time.

This takes self-discipline. If he works with slackers, they will not appreciate his diligence. It will make them feel guilty. They will look for ways to defame him. If his employer is convicted by his godly life, the employer might want to believe their tales. It takes the grace of God to endure such wrongful suffering.

But the Bible offers comfort in such a situation. Peter says, "This is thankworthy" (1 Peter 2:19).

"But let none of you suffer as a murderer, or as a thief, or as an evildoer, or as a busybody in other men's matters. Yet if any man suffer as a Christian, let him not be ashamed; but let him glorify God on this behalf" (1 Peter 4:15, 16). The Christian should not be ashamed even if he is fired for doing what is right. Whatever reproach we suffer, we take it patiently. In fact, we should expect reproach. It is our calling (1 Peter 2:21).

## 3. The Christian Employee Desires to Please His Master

"With good will doing service, as to the Lord, and not to men" involves the way we feel about our work. Did you ever get disgusted because someone was far too picky? Did you ever get frustrated because you were not sure that you were capable of satisfying your employer? Sometimes these circumstances present us with the greatest opportunity to magnify God.

Do not allow yourself to be intimidated. Be enthusiastic about doing things the way the person you are working for wants it. If he is unreasonable, be frank with him. Tell him you do not feel that you are capable of doing the job to his satisfaction. Assure him that you are willing to try. Acknowledging your weakness may call forth a more understanding acceptance of your ability. He may even commend you in the end. On the other hand, if you proudly proclaim your ability, he will likely look for flaws to prove to you your humanity. Be humble and God will exalt you. Be proud and God will humble you.

"Exhort servants to be obedient unto their own masters, and to please them well in all things; not answering again" (Titus 2:9). Christian employees do not talk back. When they make a mistake, they do not try to hide it. They acknowledge it and make the necessary amends.

People can soon tell if we are more interested in pleasing ourselves than we are in pleasing others. The selfishness of the present generation makes the Christian employee shine much brighter. He is in great demand because he can be trusted.

We always feel better about our work when we do it with goodwill. We enjoy better health. Others enjoy being around us and working with us. When we are working for Jesus and doing our best, we need not be ashamed of anything. We can be confident that God will reward us if no one else does.

*4. The Christian Employee Respects His Employer*

"Let as many servants as are under the yoke count their own masters worthy of all honour, that the name of God and his doctrine be not blasphemed" (1 Timothy 6:1). An employee is not normally under a yoke unless he has signed a contract. Usually he is free to leave one job and take up another. This does not encourage attachment or even dedication to an employer.

There is, however, a Biblical principle that the Christian needs to express in the labor field. This text does not say that the master must be worthy of all honor, but it says that the servant must count him worthy. This requires us to keep focused on the good qualities of the master.

Every employer has some noteworthy qualities. Think about those things. Promote your employer. When someone begins to complain about something, you can say, "But you're forgetting about the time he showed up and did that job himself that we did not want to do." Or you might be able to say, "Yes, and what do you think you would be paid if you were working for Sam instead?"

We live in a very negative atmosphere. People find fault with the President, with local officials, with church leaders. The Christian must be careful not to imbibe the same critical spirit. Learn the value of promoting others. Point out the good in the one being degraded. This is especially valuable as it relates to the boss. Count him worthy of all honor. You will be blessed for your efforts.

Who then is a faithful and wise servant, whom his lord hath made ruler over his household, to give them meat in due season? Blessed is that servant, whom his lord when he cometh shall find so doing. Verily I say unto you, That he shall make him ruler over all his goods. But and if that evil servant shall say in his heart, My lord delayeth his coming; and shall begin to smite his fellowservants, and to eat and drink with the drunken; the lord of that servant shall come in a day when he looketh not for him, and in an hour that he is not aware of, and shall cut him asunder, and appoint him his portion with the hypocrites: there shall be weeping and gnashing of teeth.

*Matthew 24:45—51*